North America

The North American continent has every biome and much diversity. Diversity in nature means that there are a lot of different life forms. Many of the plants and animals will be familiar and some will be surprising. We will visit the indigenous tribes of the Guna, Navajo and Inuit who live in the Tropical Forest, the Desert and the Polar Regions. The Cajun culture is native to the Wetlands of the Bayou. The Amish people of the Temperate Forest live a simple life in harmony with nature. We'll visit some people who are probably a lot like you who live in the Grasslands of Iowa and the Mountains in Canada. This book is a place for you to collect your research and study of the continent.
Have fun!

Exploring the biomes of North America

THE AMAZING
North American Adventures
of

My Name _____

About Me

My portrait

_____

_____

_____

_____

_____

_____

_____

Tape in your folded map of North America here

North America

Here you will find a list of icons and their meanings. These will show up throughout your book to guide your research and activities. You may find different ways to research, and different tools. These are the same icons that you will find on your biome cards.

 Temperate Forest

 Wetlands

 Tropical Forest

 Mountains

 Grasslands

 Polar Region

 Desert

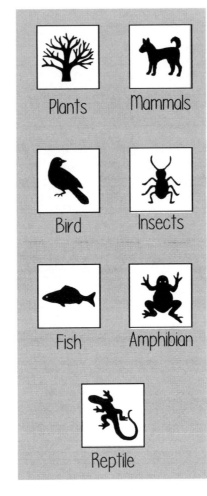

Plants Mammals

Bird Insects

Fish Amphibian

Reptile

 Shelter   People

 Food   Culture

Clothing

Transportation

Here are some supplies you will need:

 ruler

 colored pencils

 chalk

 pencil

 glue

 reference books

 internet

Let's begin in the Temperate Forest!

★ Lancaster, Pennsylvania

The Temperate Forest

This biome gets plenty of rain. There are seasons. This biome has many trees. Some trees lose their leaves in the winter. Animals here find plenty of food and shelter.

Hallo! Hoe gaat het? My name is Abram, and I live in Pennsylvania, on an Amish farm in the Temperate Forest. Please stay with me and my family on our farm, and I'll show you around!

A Day In The Life Of Abram

Use the word bank to finish this story about a typical day on an Amish farm

When the sun comes up, our rooster crows. But in the _____,

it is still dark, so I wake up before the rooster! I am awake at 7

to do my chores before school. My older brothers chop wood

for Mam (mother) to use when she cooks on the _____ .

It is my duty to feed the animals, and my sister Rachel collects eggs

from the chicken coop. I feed the _____ .

My favorite thing to do is chase the pigs!

While we do chores, Mam cooks us breakfast. Each morning,

we eat _____ . We pray together as a family

in the morning, evening and before each meal.

In the spring, my brothers, sisters and I walk to school.

But in the winter, when it is _____,

Dat (father) will drive us to school in a _____.

At school, we learn in a one-room schoolhouse. All of my friends

are from big families like me. There are about 14 families in our school!

When school is over, my brothers, sisters and I go home and do

our homework and chores. My sisters help mam prepare the supper,

I feed the _____ again,

and my brothers help Dat with the farm. In the spring and fall,

they help him to_____ or _____;

in the summer, they mow the lawn!

When it's time for supper, we eat the _____ that Mam and sisters

have prepared. After supper, my sisters wash the dishes,

then we read and play games or music.

When it gets dark, we use _____ for light, because

we do not use electricity.

When Dat says it's time for bed, I get ready for sleep then blow out my candle.

Goedenacht!

Abram's sister, Martha, washes the family laundry and hangs to dry in the sunshine. The family laundry is now clean and dry.

What will Abram and Martha wear today?

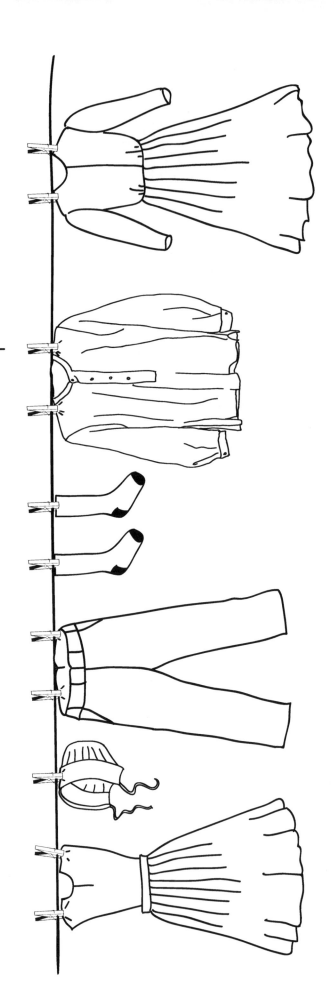

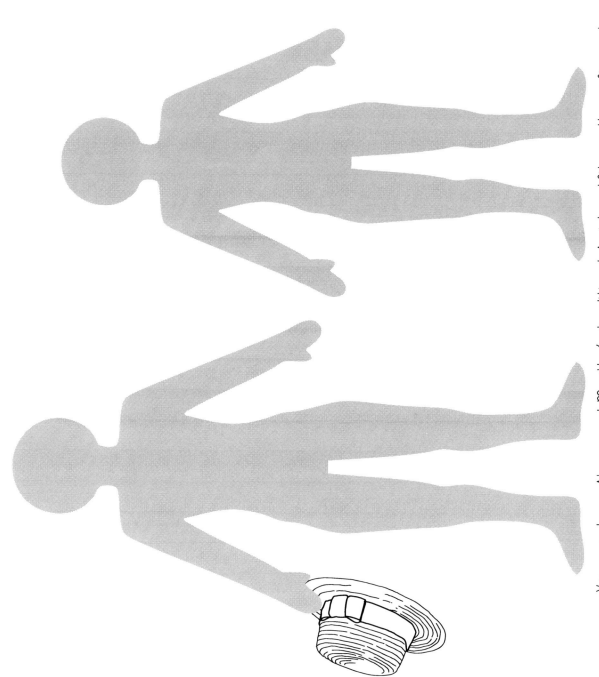

You can draw Abram and Martha's traditional Amish outfits on these figures!

Abram wants to take you on an adventure!

Trace the path you take on the map found on the next page.

 Go out the back door of Abram's house. Don't let the screen door slam. The baby is asleep.

 Walk between the barn and the garden.

 Walk between the rows of corn. Watch out for the rooster. He will chase you if you run.

 Find the path into the woods. The birds raise an alarm, telling all the animals about you.

 Walk until you find the stream. Cross over the stream to the other side.

 Follow the stream until you come to some tracks in the sand.
What kind of animal made those tracks?

 Keep following the stream. You scare a flock of really big birds into the trees.
Abram knows what they are but he won't say.

 Keep following the stream until you come to a fence.
Jump over the fence into the pasture. Jump back over the stream to the other side.

 Walk around the cows until you come to another fence.
There is a bull inside a pen. Don't go inside! Walk west and go around the pen.

 Go south when you get to the corner of the pen. Some men are working on a barn.
Many friends have come to help with a "barn raising." You and Abram help carry some boards.

 When it starts to get dark, you follow the road southwest until you come to Abram's house.
As you come inside, you smell dinner cooking.
It's biscuits and chicken and vegetables from the garden.

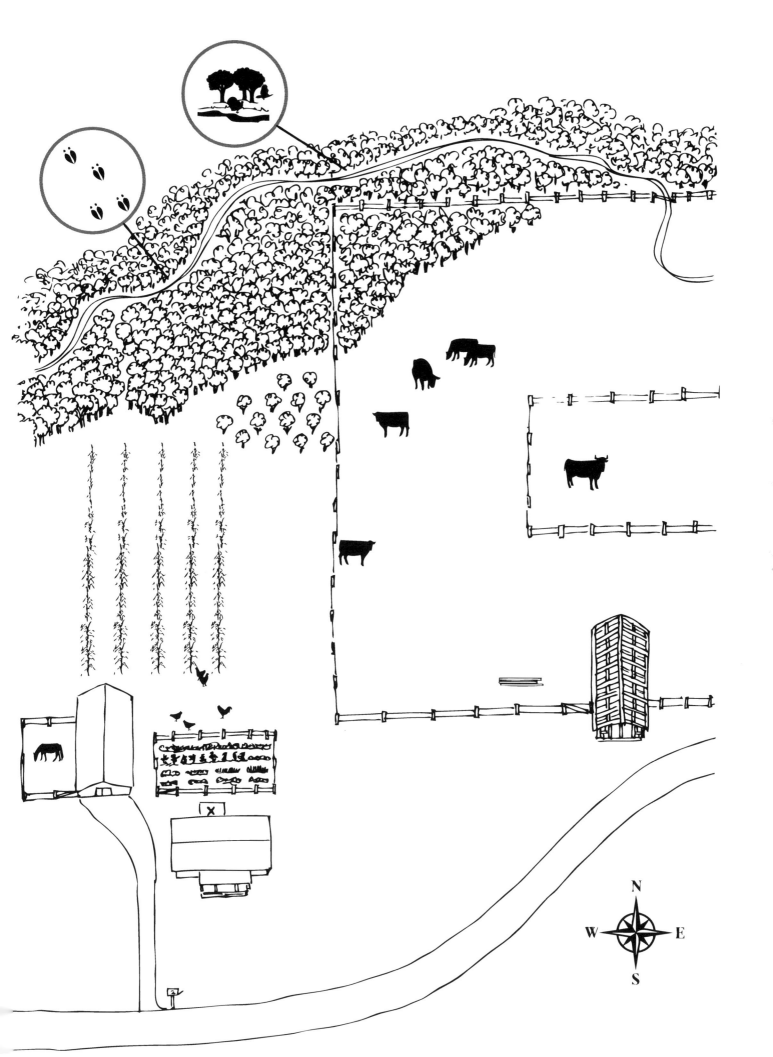

Parts of a Turkey

Fill in the diagram. Then draw in the biome around the turkey.
Color the turkey by looking at the card and noticing its markings.

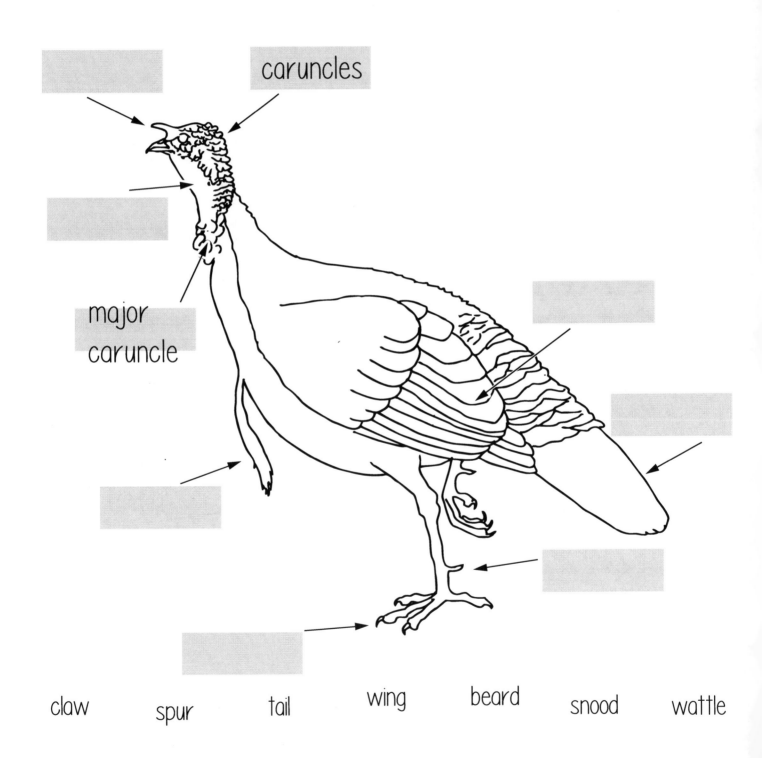

caruncles

major
caruncle

claw   spur   tail   wing   beard   snood   wattle

Animal Research

Choose an animal of the Temperate Forest of North America.
You can pick from your animals cards if you like.
Draw and write about this animal.

Animal name

Class

Biome

_____   _____   _____

_____

_____

_____

_____

_____

_____

Progression of a Rotting Log

Locate these members of the Rotting Log Ecosystem by drawing a line from their image to their location on the log.

Black Carpenter
Ant

Eastern Hercules
Beetle

Hairy Cushion
Mushroom

Yellow-red
Gill Polypore

Longhorn
Beetle Larva

Coral
Fungus

A fallen log on the forest floor is a perfect spot for scavengers and decomposers to get to work. Study the log for the changes these species make to the log over time.

Can you find other insects or plants in this miniature ecosystem? Can you imagine other animals that may live here? Look for examples and add new animals. Draw them in the blank circles and draw a line from their circle to their location on the log!

Draw a baby deer in his Temperate Forest Biome

Use the next page to draw a deer. Draw the gray lines in pencil. Use a pen for the black lines.
Then erase the pencil lines and color your drawing!

A doe leaves her baby in a safe place while she goes out to find food.
The baby deer has no smell that would attract a predator.
Draw tall grass behind and beside the baby to hide it.

BIG & small

{ Each of these native plants of the Temperate Forests of North America is a different size. Use the information from the chart below to draw them!

COMMON NAME		HEIGHT
red raspberry		6 FT.
ostrich fern		3 FT.
fly agaric		3 IN.
wild plum tree	How tall is the plum tree?	☐ FT.

20

15

10

5

0
FEET

ostrich fern   fly agaric   wild plum tree   wild red raspberry

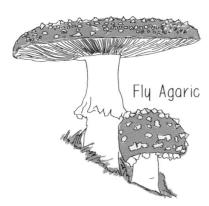

Fly Agaric

Ostritch Fern

Wild Red Raspberry

How Do They Interact?

Fungus growing in the Temperate Forest has a network of root-like rhizomes in the ground. It takes energy from the trees that use the sun's energy to make food. In return, the fungus acts as extra roots for the trees and helps to gather water and minerals that trees need to make food. The way that they interact is called symbiosis (symbiōsis).

Draw a picture of the tree and the fungus in the box where they belong.

➕ [ ]

⬅ gives water and minerals to

➡ gives energy to

[ ] ➕

_____   _____

How does the fungus help the trees? _____

_____

_____

_____

How do the trees help the fungus? _____

_____

_____

_____

Temperate Forest Food Chain

Start by drawing or writing the name of the maple leaves in the top circle for the plant that gets its energy from the sun. Follow the arrows to show the caterpillar of the luna moth that eats the leaves of the maple tree.. Then, the animal that eats that animal. What predator eats the animal that eats the animal who has eaten the plant? Draw or write it in the next circle. Use the animals illustrated.

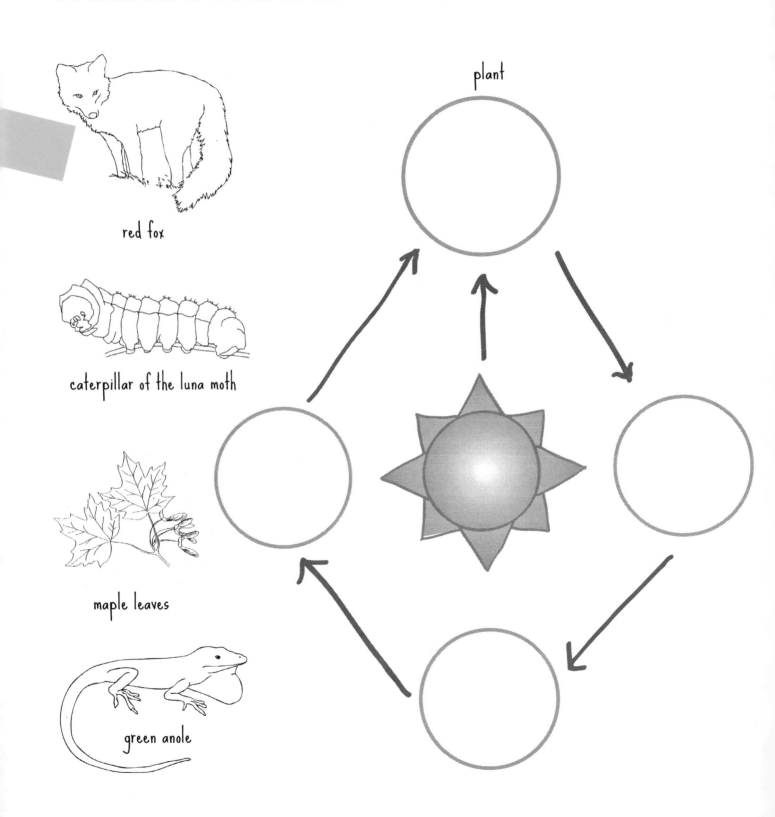

red fox

caterpillar of the luna moth

maple leaves

green anole

plant

Animal Research

Choose an animal of the Temperate Forest of North America.
You can pick from your animals cards if you like.
Draw and write about this animal.

Animal name   *Class*   *Biome*

_____   _____   _____

_____

_____

_____

_____

_____

_____

_____

What has happened to the forest?

When the first settlers came to North America from Europe, they were amazed to find so much forest. In Europe, much of the forest had been cut for a long time. The settlers began to clear land for farming. They used trees for fuel, fences and homes. This did not make a big difference until more and more settlers came.

In the 1800's, a lot of land in the eastern United States was cleared for farming as the number of people grew and they needed to be fed. In the early 1900's, a lot of trees were cut for lumber to build and manufacture things. People began to worry that all of the forest might be gone if they did not do something. So, they began to save forests and plant trees.

Today, we plant more trees than we cut. Make a graph to show what happened to the forest.

From 1630 until 1710, settlers came from Europe to find about 1,040 million acres of forest.

- Find the year 1710 on the chart and go up the graph to the number 1,040. Find a circle where those two lines intersect. This is your starting point.

- In 1750, more settlers came and cleared more land for farming until there were 1,020 million acres. Make a circle where 1750 and 1,020 intersect.

- In 1790, there were only 1,000 million, or billion, acres left. Make a mark at 1,000 on the line for the year 1790.

- In 1830, trees were cut for fields and also for lumber to build things. Make a mark at 960 million acres.

- In 1870, more trees were cut until there were only 860 million acres.

- In 1910, machines cut and built things out of wood faster and better. There were only 700 million acres left.

- In 1950, People began to save forests and plant trees. The amount of forest grew to 720 million acres.

- In 1990, more forest were saved and more trees were planted to make 740 million acres.

- In 2010, there were 750 million acres of forest in the United States. Make a mark between 740 and 760 on the last line.

- Use a ruler to make a straight line from each mark to the next. This graph shows how the amount of forest in the United States changed over time. It also shows how people can make choices that protect nature.

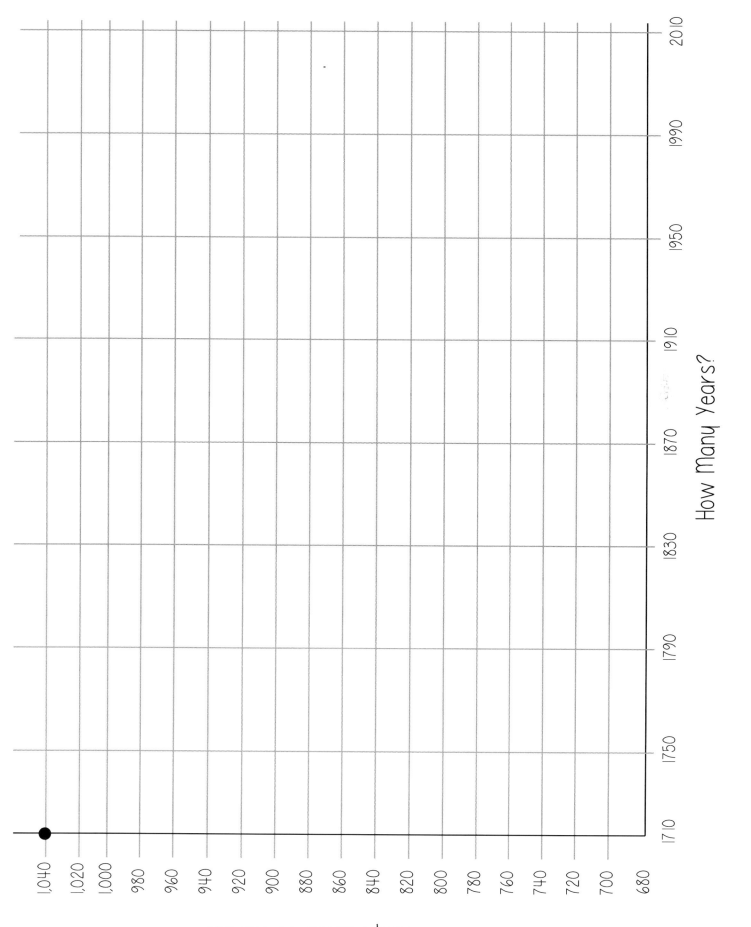

How Many Years?

How Many Millions Of Acres?

1,040 1,020 1,000 980 960 940 920 900 880 860 840 820 800 780 760 740 720 700 680

1710 1750 1790 1830 1870 1910 1950 1990 2010

Things I know now about the Temperate Forest of North America

_____

_____

_____

_____

_____

_____

Things I wonder about the Temperate Forest of North America

_____

_____

_____

_____

_____

_____

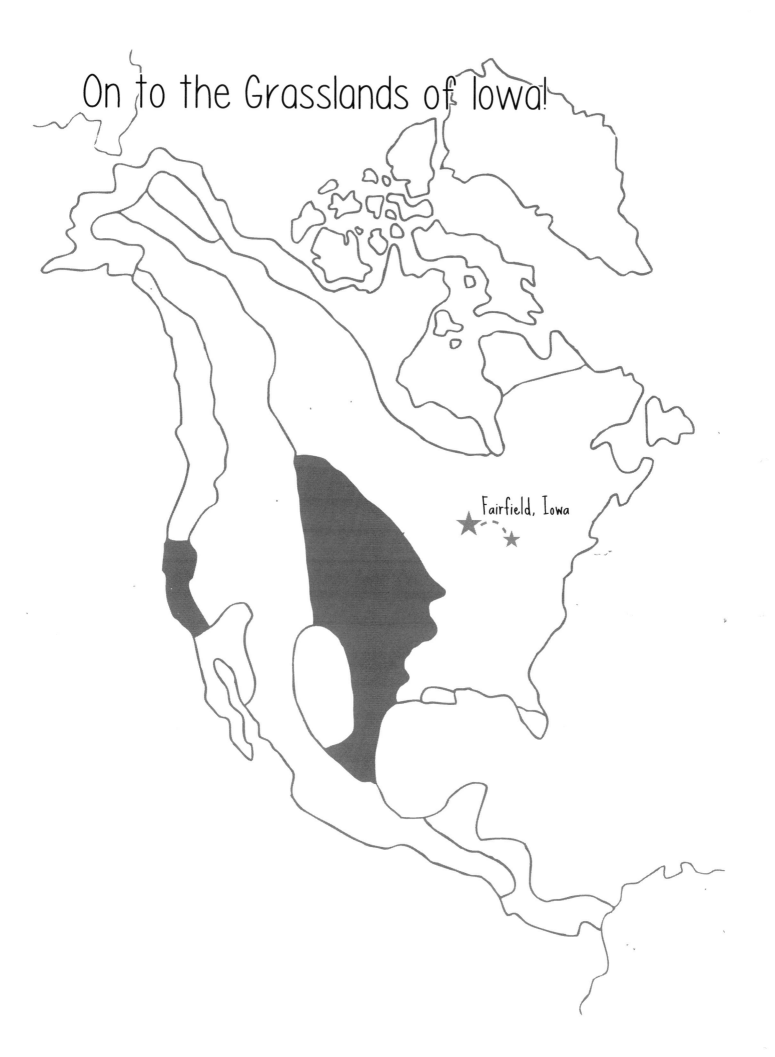

On to the Grasslands of Iowa!

Fairfield, Iowa

The Grasslands

This biome gets some rain. Winters can be very cold with lots of snow. Grasses grow here but not many trees. Some animals eat grass and live in herds. Others live underground.

A Day at The Iowa State Fair

Use the word bank to finish this story about
a great day with Emma at the fair!

| to milk | jam and jelly | cattle | crops, food and crafts | ferris wheel | farm |
| eggs | Iowa State Fair | memory quilt | Farmers | butter | midway | on-a-stick | blue ribbon |

In the morning, I wake up early to help feed the animals and _____ our

cows. My family eats a hearty breakfast of fresh_____, bacon,

biscuits, and homemade _____, because we need lots of energy.

Today is a very special day, because my family is heading to the

_____! There are many competitions, and we are

entering several of them. My parents grow corn and tomatoes, and I'm sure they'll win

for best taste! I helped my mother cut up my sister's old baby clothes to make a

_____ for the fair, and I'm entering my cow Bessie in the Jersey

_____ competition.

We load everything into our truck and trailer, and drive to the fair. Even though it's

early, the whole place is buzzing with activity. _____

and families from all over the state have come to set up booths and show off their

prized _____.

My sister Jessa gawks at the cow statue made entirely out of

_____. It looks like Bessie!

My mother's quilt is already on display. It looks beautiful. We walk through the

_____ and see all the booths selling food and crafts. We buy lunch and

make sure to save room for our new favorite, funnel cake

_____! In the event hall, our tomatoes get an

honorable mention for best taste. Jessa and I can't wait to brag about our prize-

winning tomatoes at the farmer's market when we get home!

In the afternoon, Bessie's event is judged. She doesn't win the

_____, but I think she's the best in the show. At night, the

whole fair glitters with lights from the rides. Jessa and I ride the

_____ and eat fresh-made ice cream. It's late when our family

packs everything up and drives back home to the _____, and

Jessa and I fall asleep on the way home. I smile the whole way--

it's been a very special day!

Market Math

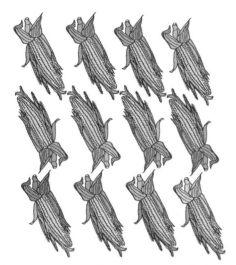

12 ears of corn = 1 peck

1 peck of corn is $6.00

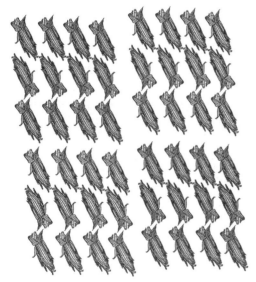

4 pecks of corn = 1 bushel

1 pint of tomatoes
is $3.00

In the summer, my whole family helps pick and bag sweet corn and tomatoes to sell at the farmers market on Saturdays. It takes us two days to pick enough corn and tomatoes to sell!

Do the math!

Use the next page to work on these problems. Then put your answers in the boxes below.

Level 1: Mr. Breamer comes to our booth. He wants to buy 16 ears of corn. A peck holds 12 ears of corn. If he buys one peck, how many more ears does he need to buy?

Last week, we sold 21 pecks of corn. The week before, we sold 15. How many more pecks of corn did we sell last week?

Level 2: We sell tomatoes for $3 a pint. We sell corn for $6 a peck. When Miss Walker comes to the booth, she wants to buy 4 pints of tomatoes and 2 pecks of corn. How much does Miss Walker owe?

Level 3: We divide our sweet corn into pecks, and each peck holds 12 ears of corn. We sell a peck of corn for six dollars. How much do we charge for each ear?

Last Saturday, we sold 12 pecks of corn and 64 pints of tomatoes. How many ears did we sell?

How much did we make from the corn?

How much did we make in total?

This Way to the Corn Maze!

Some farmers plant a maze into their land with corn plants! When the corn has matured in the fall, they put up signs to attract visitors to the farm. People come and pay a fee to find their way through the maze.

Exit

Entrance

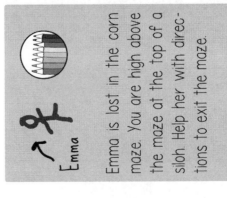

Emma is lost in the corn maze. You are high above the maze at the top of a silo. Help her with directions to exit the maze.

Trace the path she should take with your finger, or color a path for her with a colored pencil.

Parts of a Corn Plant

Read about the adaptations of the corn plant. Study the illustration and use the word bank to fill in the diagram.

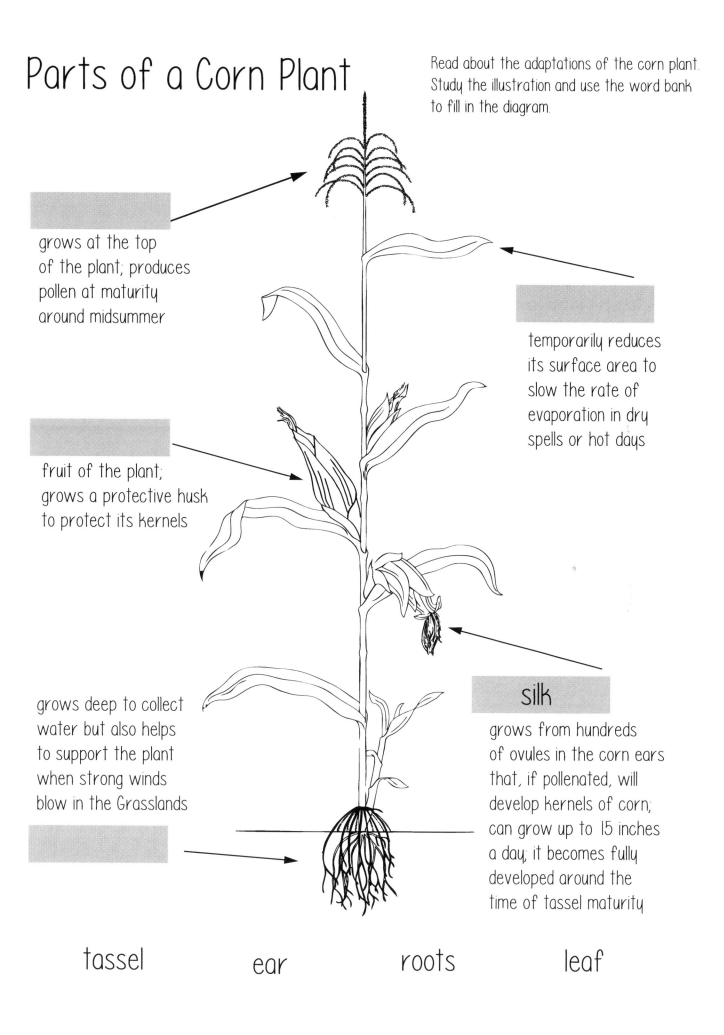

grows at the top of the plant; produces pollen at maturity around midsummer

temporarily reduces its surface area to slow the rate of evaporation in dry spells or hot days

fruit of the plant; grows a protective husk to protect its kernels

grows deep to collect water but also helps to support the plant when strong winds blow in the Grasslands

silk

grows from hundreds of ovules in the corn ears that, if pollenated, will develop kernels of corn; can grow up to 15 inches a day; it becomes fully developed around the time of tassel maturity

tassel   ear   roots   leaf

Help Emma make a chart of how the corn grows.
Make a mark at the top of each plant. Use a ruler
to connect each mark. You made a graph!

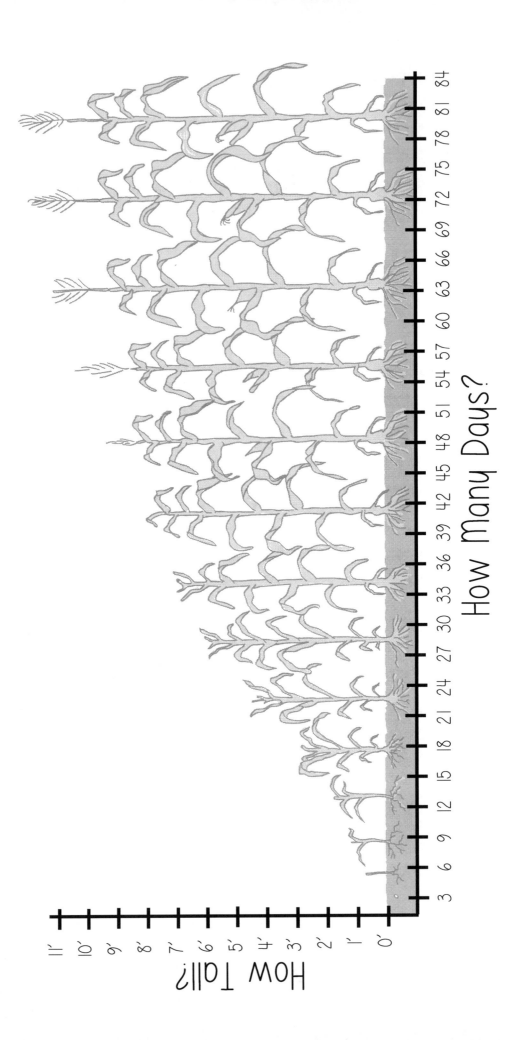

How Many Days?

How Tall?

3 6 9 12 15 18 21 24 27 30 33 36 39 42 45 48 51 54 57 60 63 66 69 72 75 78 81 84

11' 10' 9' 8' 7' 6' 5' 4' 3' 2' 1' 0'

How does the corn grow?

Emma helps her dad observe how the new seed he planted grows. She watches a particular plant at the end of one of the rows. Every day, she goes out and measures the plant with a tape measure. She records the measurement and the date. She also makes notes about how many leaves it has at first and when the second node appears. She watches to see when the first tassel comes and when the silk shows out of the ear of corn. That means it is ripe.

Look at the line you made between day 3 and 48. Does it go up at a steep slope? What does the steep slope mean?

_____

_____

_____

How many days does it take to grow an ear of corn?

_____

_____

Look at the line above the plants as they got older. Is the slope more or less steep? Why do you think the plant stopped growing so tall?

_____

_____

_____

_____

_____

The very colorful Greater Prairie Chicken

  Color and label the parts of the bird and draw in what he is pecking!
Check the cards for coloring cues.

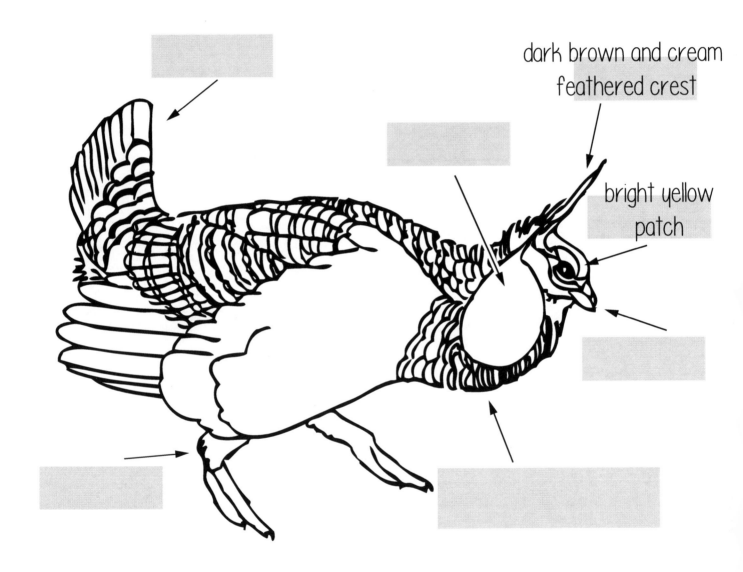

dark brown and cream
feathered crest

bright yellow
patch

brown, cream and deep dark brown feathers   yellow legs and feet

bright yellow-orange throat sac   brown bill   brown short rounded tail

Creating a Memory Quilt

Reusing fabric from old clothes is a great way to make a quilt. To begin, each piece of fabric is cut into a shape. By stitching the shapes together, you create a collection of memories. You can arrange the pieces in many ways, but Emma wants to create a "Tumbling Block" quilt. Design the quilt by coloring in each diamond differently to reveal the pattern.

Powerful Weather

The grassland is a wide-open country where the weather can change quickly. This is a perfect environment for tornadoes to develop and travel quickly. Tornadoes occur all over the world, but North America gets the most. The worst hit area is a stretch of land known as 'Tornado Alley' that extends from Texas to South Dakota. This area is particularly vulnerable because it's where the dry air from the Rocky Mountains intersects with the warm, moist air from the Gulf and the cold Arctic air from the north. The mix of the three provides the perfect conditions to create storms powerful enough to turn into tornadoes.

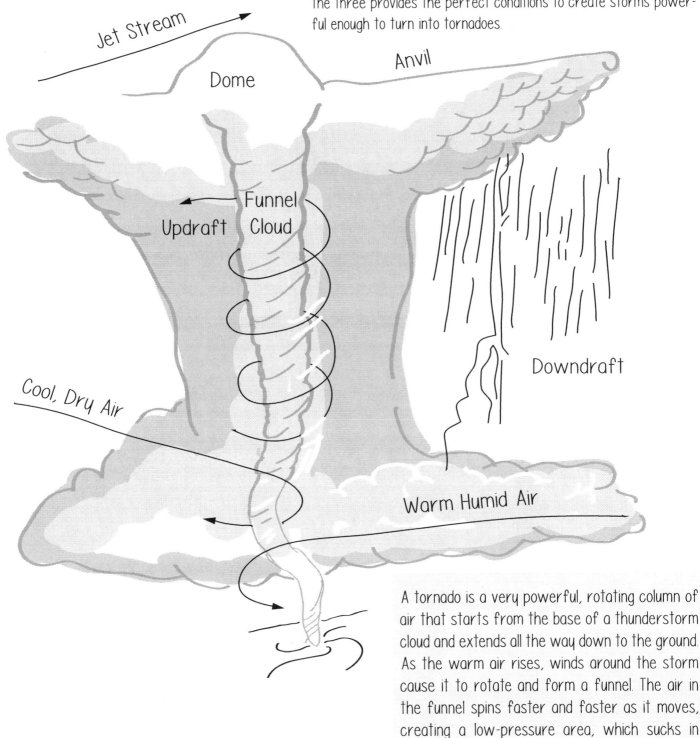

Jet Stream

Dome

Anvil

Funnel Cloud

Updraft

Downdraft

Cool, Dry Air

Warm Humid Air

A tornado is a very powerful, rotating column of air that starts from the base of a thunderstorm cloud and extends all the way down to the ground. As the warm air rises, winds around the storm cause it to rotate and form a funnel. The air in the funnel spins faster and faster as it moves, creating a low-pressure area, which sucks in even more air and sometimes even objects!

Draw a tornado in this scene!

We use this underground shelter as a root cellar and a storm cellar. Root cellars are good for keeping food supplies at a low temperature and steady humidity. They keep food from freezing during the winter and keep food cool during the summer months to prevent spoiling. In the fall, after harvesting, we will put up vegetables and canned goods in the root cellar. In the spring months, March to June, we know that we have a safe, underground place to batten down during tornado season.

Prairie Dog Town

The morning air is cool and there is dew on the grass as the first furry head peeks out of the dark burrow. It is the male prairie dog. He is in charge of keeping his family safe. He smells the air and looks sharply to the left and right. He crawls on top of the mound at the entrance to his burrow, where he can see farther. A female prairie dog and some pups come out of the burrow. Then, two more females and more pups. They start to feed on the nearby grass, standing up to chew as they look around. Prairie dogs have to be very alert. There are many animals that would eat them. The prairie dog pups play. They nip at one another's tails and run off to be chased. The father is watchful. He sees something coming across the prairie. He gives a warning yip. All of the prairie dogs look and scamper close to the burrow. Prairie dog families build their burrows close to each other. This is called a town. Prairie dogs in the town run to their burrows. Several prong horn deer have wandered into the town. The prairie dogs give a yip that means "deer." All of the prairie dogs relax and go back to eating grass. The deer graze, too.

One prairie dog jumps into the air, lands on his bottom and gives a short bark. The prairie dogs next to him do the same thing. Prairie dogs all over town do it. Then, it stops and they go back to eating. The females groom some of the pups by biting on their fur. Other pups want to be groomed, too. They rub up against the females. All of the females take care of all of the pups in the burrow. The prong horn deer stand alert. The prairie dogs freeze to look and smell for danger.

There is a bark from across the town. This bark means, "Badger coming!" Everyone goes quickly down into the burrow. A badger comes into the prairie dog town. The badger has sharp claws and can dig up a prairie dog burrow. He eats prairie dogs. The family of prairie dogs huddle together inside the nursery chamber, waiting silently. They hear a scratching right above them. The male gives a signal, and everyone goes quickly towards the back door. The badger digs deeper and pokes his head down into the hole, just as the family comes out of the back door and scampers away to safety. They will stay in an abandoned burrow until it is safe to come home.

Why do you think the prairie dogs all do the "jump-yip"?

_____

_____

Why do you think the prairie dogs choose the nursery chamber to hide from the badger?

_____

_____

Imagine that you are one of the animals in the story. You might be the male, a female or one of the pups. You might be a deer or a badger. Imagine that you are that animal and tell the story as the animal you have chosen. What happened to you?

_____

_____

_____

_____

_____

_____

_____

_____

_____

_____

_____

_____

_____

Draw a Prarie Dog on top of his mound.

Draw the gray lines in pencil. Use a pen for the black lines.
Then erase the pencil lines and color your drawing!

Draw other prairie dogs in the burrow if you like.

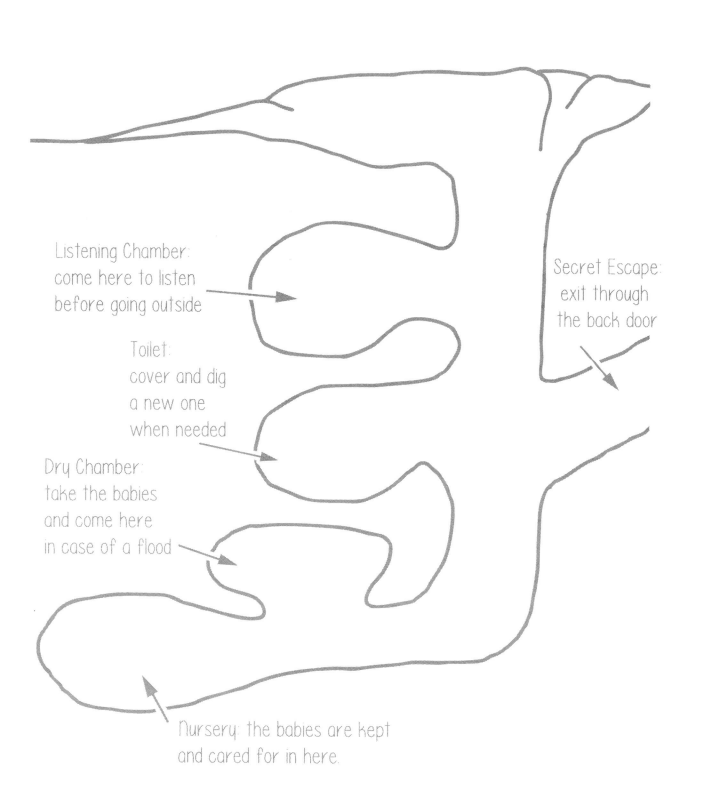

Listening Chamber: come here to listen before going outside

Toilet: cover and dig a new one when needed

Dry Chamber: take the babies and come here in case of a flood

Secret Escape: exit through the back door

Nursery: the babies are kept and cared for in here.

Animal Research

Choose an animal from the Grasslands of North America.
You can pick from your animals cards if you like.
Draw and write about this animal.

Animal name   Class   Biome

_____   _____   _____

_____

_____

_____

_____

_____

_____

How Do They Interact?

Find two animals in the Grasslands of North America. One should be a predator and the other should be its prey. Draw them in the correct boxes and write their names underneath.

prey   predator

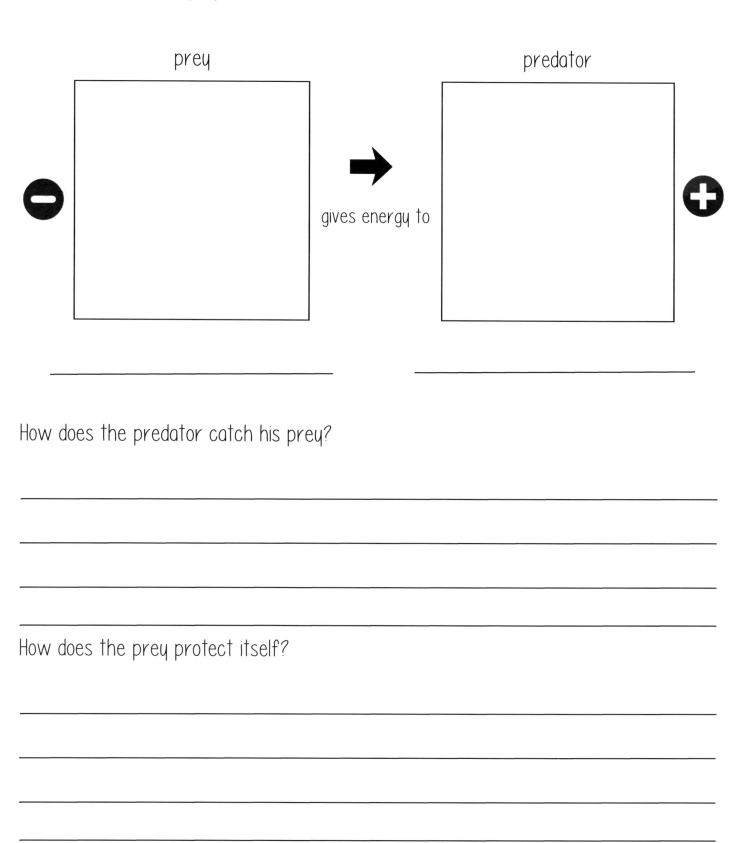

gives energy to

How does the predator catch his prey?

_____

_____

_____

How does the prey protect itself?

_____

_____

_____

Grassland Food Chain

Start by drawing or writing the grass plant in the top circle for the thing that gets its energy from the sun. Follow the arrows to draw the animal that eats the plant. Then, the animal that eats that animal. What eats that animal? Draw or write it in the next circle. Use the animals illustrated.

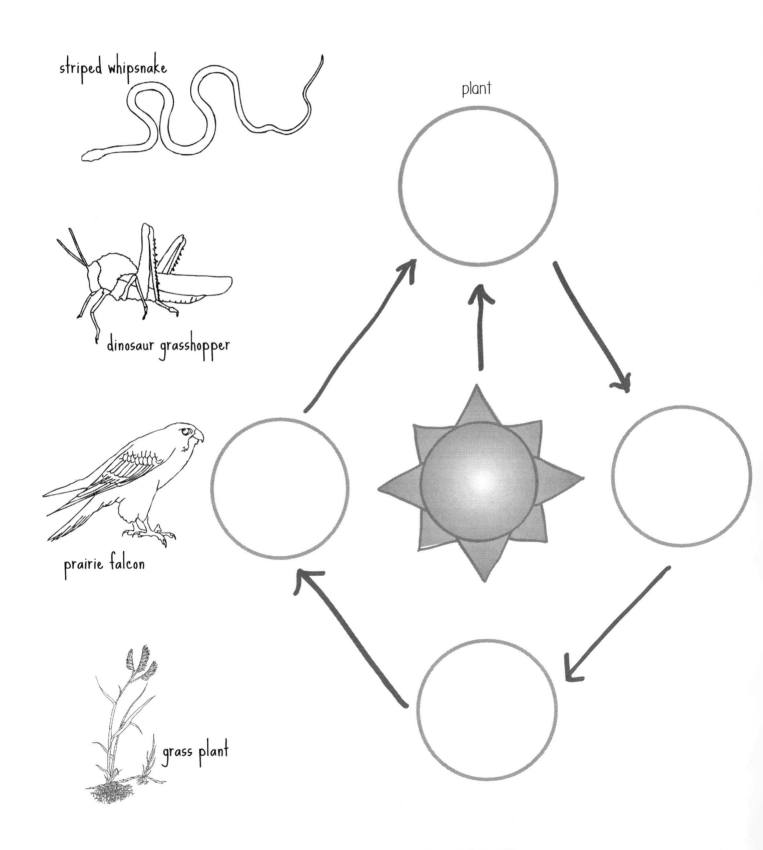

striped whipsnake

dinosaur grasshopper

prairie falcon

grass plant

plant

Plant Research

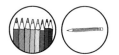

Choose a plant from the Grasslands of North America.
You can pick from your cards if you like. Draw and write about this plant.

Plant name

Class

Biome

Things I know now about the Grasslands of North America

_____
_____
_____
_____
_____
_____

Things I wonder about the Grasslands of North America

_____
_____
_____
_____
_____

Now, to the Wetlands of Louisiana!

Chauvin, Louisiana

The Wetlands

This biome is covered in water most of the time.
It can be a swamp or a place near the sea.
Plants grow up out of the water. Most animals
swim, dive or have long legs to stand on.

Bonjou! My name is René. {Ruh-nay} My family is Cajun and we live in the Wetlands of Lousiana, but we call it the bayou! We love having company, so stay a while, and I'll show you around!

Parts of a Bald Cypress

The Bald Cypress is a large tree. The bark is gray-brown to red-brown, with a stringy texture. This tree is called 'bald' because it loses its leaves in the winter. The main trunks are surrounded by cypress knees. Knees are woody parts of the trunk sent above the normal water level. Some scientists have thought they may help in oxygenation to the tree's roots or assist in anchoring the tree in the soft, muddy soil. Use this information to fill in the diagram. When you have questions, write them down and go to a library to do some research.

needle-like leaves

branches   knees   underwater roots

A Visit with René

René wants to take you out in his pirogue {pee-rog}, a flat-bottom boat.
He keeps it on the water tied to a tree in his backyard.

✶ Begin at René's home in Chauvin.

René takes the stern so that he can steer. Together, you paddle north. You come to an island of Rosseau grass with a few trees. You see a muskrat near the shore. He's got a catfish! The sun is beginning to set on the bayou.

Go around the island and paddle back south. René says that if you stay out until dark, you might see the water look golden brown when you shine your flashlight. But it's not the water, it's the light reflected back from a hundred alligator eyes! You paddle faster. Pull back up to René's house and tie the pirogue to a tree. Go inside for some gumbo.

 Color the land in the map deep shades of green.
Read the story and trace the course you took on the map.
Make a mark where you imagine spotting the muskrat!

Navigating the Mississippi Delta

The next day, René's father has to go to the Delta to buy a new motor part for his shrimp boat. He offers to take you and René along. You go down to the docks in Chauvin, climb aboard and head south, away from town.

HOW TO USE THE MAP: Read the story and trace the course you took on the map to get to the mud lumps at Pass a Loutré.

AFTER YOUR TRIP: Name 4 animals that you saw on your visit with René.

1. _____

2. _____

3. _____

4. _____

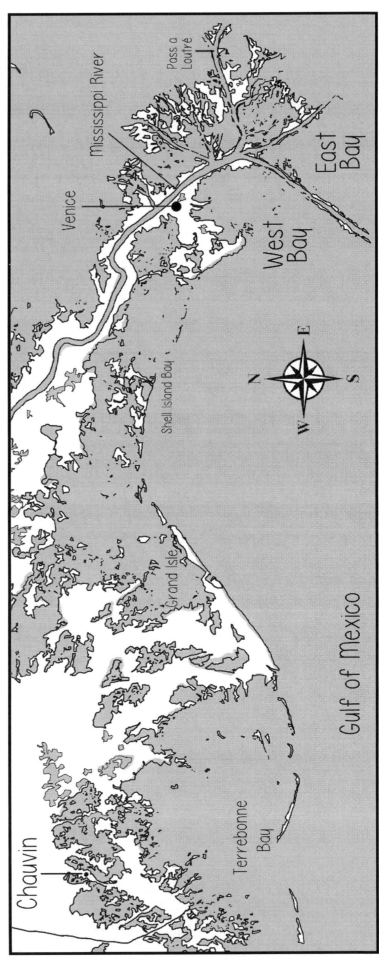

SETTING SAIL

SETTING SAIL: Find your way through the straits and around the islands to the open water of Terrebonne Bay. Go south across Terrebonne Bay, past the long barrier islands and into the Gulf of Mexico. The Gulf is so big that it looks like the ocean. Go east close to shore and keep the land in sight.

If you keep following the shoreline, you will come to Grand Isle. Then, you pass by a small group of islands in a place called Shell Bay. Continue southeast until you come to West Bay. This is where the Missisipi Delta empties into the Gulf of Mexico. It is called "bird foot" because of its shape.

MAKING HEADWAY

MAKING HEADWAY: The airboat goes south back down the Mississippi River until you get to the three forks in the river. You head east on the one that will take you to Pass a Loutré. You learn that Pass a Loutré means "pass has otter." Captain Jacques says there are not many otters left but there must have been a lot of them when the French named it.

Go south until you come to the first branch of the river. The shrimp boat is deep and must go up the river channel so that it won't get stuck on a sand bar. Turn and go north now, up the river, until you come to the main channel. Keep going north until you get to Venice.

AYE, AYE, CAPTAIN!

AYE, AYE, CAPTAIN! At the dock, you meet René's grandpère, Captain Jacques Boudreaux, who has an airboat. The motor is a fan on the deck that blows behind and pushes the light boat forward. It is a boat that won't get stuck in shallow water. He offers to take you and René fishing for speckled trout while the shrimp boat is getting repaired. You hop aboard for an adventure!

SAILING ON

SAILING ON: You look out across the water and see something swimming with its nose up. You point and shout to René and the Captain.

"It's an otter!" says René. The captain says that's a sure sign of good luck.

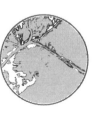

The captain gives you each a pole with a line and a hook. You put some crayfish on the hook and cast it out toward the mud lumps. A minute later, two big speckled trout flop across the deck! You and René catch six in a short time.

"That _was_ some good luck!" you say.

RETURNING TO HARBOR

RETURNING TO HARBOR: You take the same route back to Venice. René's pere is waiting and you head back to Chauvin on his shrimp boat for a dinner of fried trout and dirty rice. Everyone says "merci beacoup" for catching dinner!

Parts of a Tadpole Madtom

Fill in the diagram. Then draw in the biome around the fish.
Look on the internet or in a book to learn more!

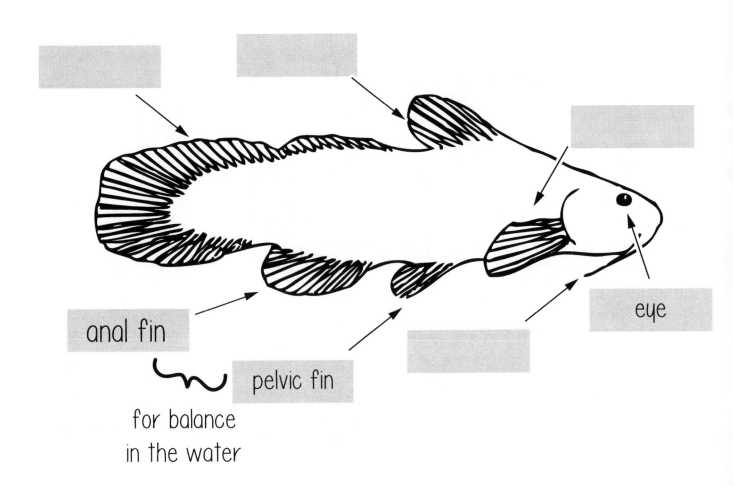

eye

anal fin

for balance
in the water

pelvic fin

barbels
work like
whiskers

dorsal fin
keeps
them upright

caudal fin
propells the fish
in the water

pectoral fin
helps to direct
left and right

Bayou Bait Shop

Here is a sketch of René's grandpère's Bait Shop. It stands above the swamp on stilts so that fisherman can drive their boats right up to the dock. Use a pencil to finish the drawing with plants, animals, people or transportaion you might find here. Color it in with your colored pencils.

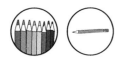

Courir de Mardi Gras, or literally, "Run of Mardi Gras" is a rural Louisiana tradition. Participants will gather to parade the roads to their neighbors homes. They will stop to entertain at the houses along the way with songs and skits. Delicious food is prepared and eaten together. All day, everyone celebrates while wearing colorful handmade costumes. The costumes often include a tall cone-shaped hat, a mask and lots of fringed fabric!

Make a Festival Costume!

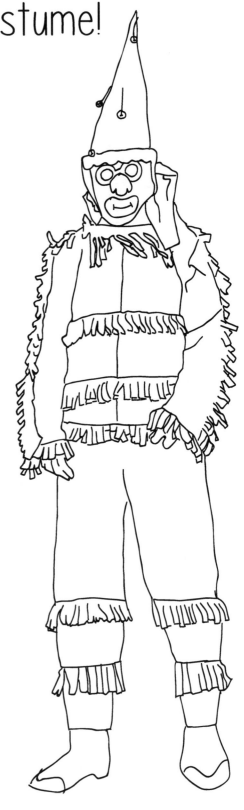

Typical Mardi Gras costumes are purple, green and gold. However, rural Mardi Gras costumes like these are any and every color, including lots of mismatched patterns adorned with fringe, ribbons and bells! Color these costumes and then create your own design on the next page.

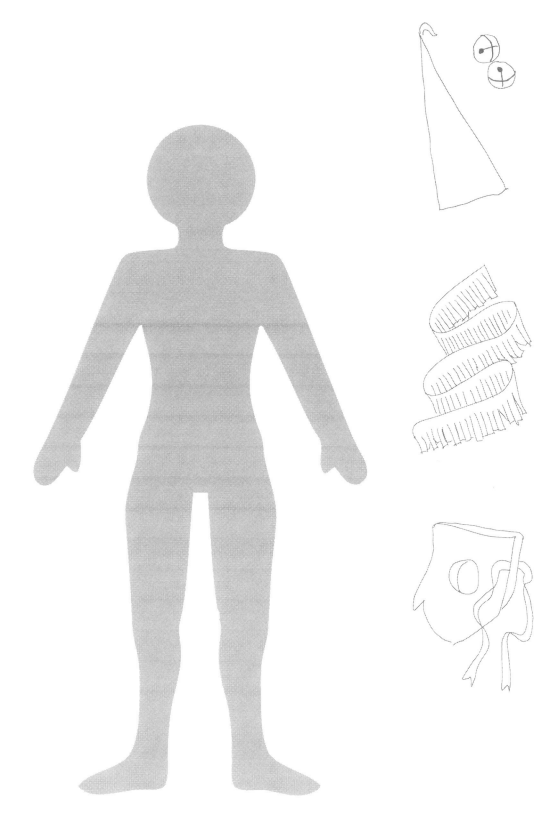

René's friend Marie has been making her own festival costume for years. She says,
"Festival costumes can be a lot of mischievous fun, because no one knows who you are!"
Make sure to design an outfit that covers every part of your body!

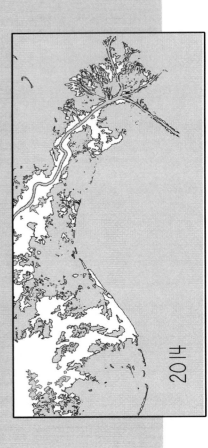

2014

In 1930, there were about 7,500 square miles of land area in the Mississippi Delta.

- Find 1930 on the chart and go up the graph to the number 7,500. Find a circle marked where those two lines intersect.

- In 1940, there were 7,300 square miles. Make a circle where 1940 and 7,300 intersect.

- In 1950, there were 7,200 square miles. Make a mark just above the 7,100 line for 1950.

- In 1960, there were 7,000 square miles. Estimate where to make your mark on the 1960 line.

- In 1970, there were 6,800 square miles. Estimate where to make your mark on the 1970 line.

- In 1980, there were only 6,100 square miles!

- In 1990, there were 5,900 square miles.

- In the year 2000, there were 5,800 square miles.

- In 2010, there were 5,500 square miles.

- Use a ruler to connect the circles. Make a prediction of how much will be left in the year 2020.

1904

How does the Mississippi Delta change?

The Mississippi River Delta formed over the last 7,000 years. It is natural for a river delta to build up sediment or soil in some places and lose it in others. In recent history, the delta has lost far more land than it has gained. Some of the land loss is due to hurricanes and climate change that makes sea levels rise. Other causes are the levees or dams along the banks that were made by people.

These levees keep the river from spreading out to areas and depositing silt carried down the river. They were built to control the river so that some areas could be used by people. As the land sinks further, the delta is more open to flooding from hurricanes. Make a graph below to see how fast it is happening.

How Many Square Miles?

	1930	1940	1950	1960	1970	1980	1990	2000	2010	2020
7,700										
7,500	●									
7,300										
7,100										
6,900										
6,700										
6,500										
6,300										
6,100										
5,900										
5,700										
5,500										
5,300										

How Many Years?

Gator Hole

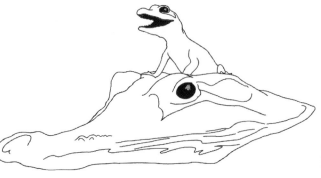

In the marsh, it is the dry season. It hasn't rained in a long time, and some of the streams are drying up. But look! Over in the sawgrass around those willow trees is a small, private pool. An alligator lives there. It swings its tail and body back and forth and moves the mud to make a hole that fills up with water. It pulls plants up that try to grow and clog up the hole. Other animals come here to live, too. There is the alligator floating on top of the water! Its eyes and nostrils poke up above the water so that it can see and breathe. It swims by moving its tail back and forth.

This is a female alligator. It is time for her to lay her eggs. She climbs up on the shore and uses her back legs to pile up mud and grass in a mound. Then she digs a hole in the top and lays about 30 eggs. She crawls along the side of the nest and pushes dirt over the eggs, being careful not to crush them. Then she goes back into the water to wait. It might take more than two months, but the mother alligator stays on guard.

One day, sounds like grunts and yelps come from inside the eggs within the mound. The mother alligator hears and comes to scratch and open up the nest. Inside the eggs, the baby alligators have a special "tooth" on their snout to break open the shell. The first egg opens and a baby alligator pops out. The mother alligator helps some of the other eggs that are moving and yelping to open. Ten baby alligators climb out of the nest. They have yellow-orange stripes. Some of the eggs are still and quiet. If the egg got too cold or too warm, the embryo inside dies. The mother alligator helps the babies to the water. They can already swim. Sometimes the mother carries them gently in her mouth. Sometimes they climb on her back. They find their own food. They eat dragonflies, grasshoppers, crayfish and small fish in their pond.

A heron on the bank looks over at the baby alligators. It has found the hole that the alligator made and finds fish here to eat. A small school of fish swim by. It grabs one in its long beak. The heron would like to taste a baby alligator, but the mother is too close. The mother alligator will stay close by, ready to protect her babies. She floats like a log in the pool. A water moccasin slithers on top of the water. Suddenly, there is a big commotion, splashing and thrashing! The alligator catches the snake in her mouth!

Another day, the baby alligators are resting on the bank, soaking up the last rays of warm sunshine. The mother alligator is a short distance away, floating in the water. A raccoon is peeking at them from behind the grass. The baby alligators look like a good meal for him. He pounces to catch one. The baby alligators yelp loudly in alarm. The mother suddenly splashes and lunges out of the water onto the bank. The raccoon backs quickly away. The mother stands guard over the babies until she is sure that the raccoon has gone. Out of the ten, maybe one or two of her babies will grow large enough to be safe on their own. It is a dangerous world for baby alligators, even with their mother to protect them.

Imagine that you are one of the animals in the story. You might be the mother alligator, a baby alligator, a heron, a water moccasin or a raccoon. Imagine that you are that animal and tell the story the way that it happened to you.

_____

_____

_____

_____

_____

_____

_____

_____

_____

_____

_____

_____

_____

_____

_____

_____

Draw an alligator in his Wetland Biome

Use a pencil to draw the gray lines. Draw the black lines with a pen. Then erase the pencil lines.

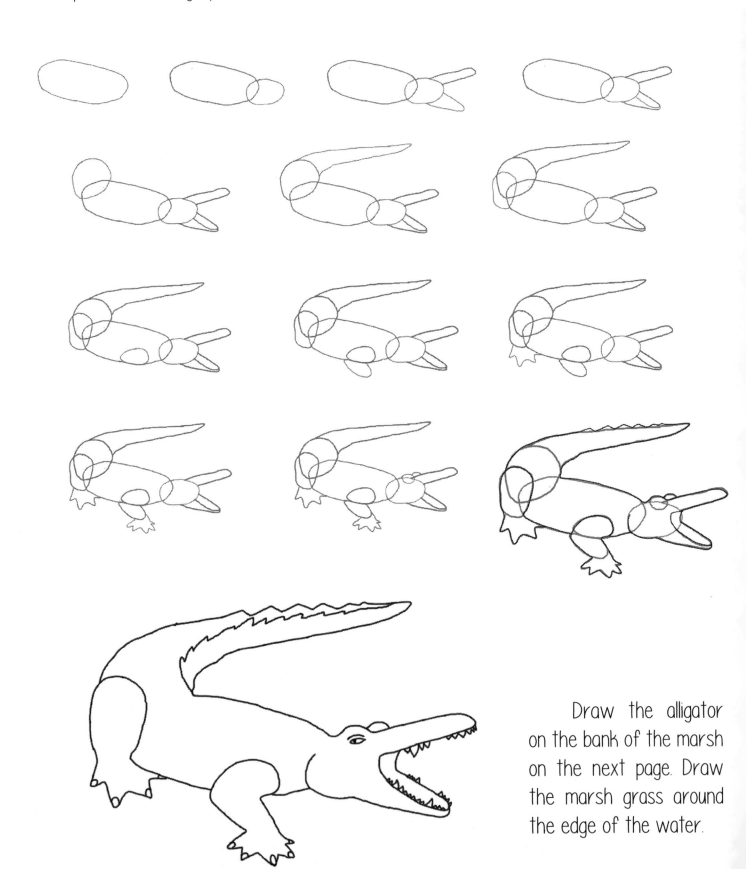

Draw the alligator on the bank of the marsh on the next page. Draw the marsh grass around the edge of the water.

Adaptation Matching

The Wetlands are flooded with water. Draw a line from the animal to the description of how it lives in its biome. Write a description of how the egret has adapted to life in the Wetlands..

snail kite

This animal can swim very far underwater. It has webs between its toes. It eats the grasses that are plentiful in the marsh.

American alligator

This bird has a hooked beak that is designed to get apple snails out of their shells. It has talons to grab the shells out of the water.

marsh rice rat

This animal has bulging eyes and nostrils that point up at the end of its snout. This helps it hide in the water while still breathing and looking for prey. It looks like a floating log.

egret

_____

_____

_____

_____

_____

Animal Research

Choose an animal of the Wetlands of North America.
You can pick from your animals cards if you like. Draw and write about this animal.

Animal name

Class

Biome

Wetlands Food Chain

Start by drawing or writing the name of the Rosseau grass in the circle for the plant that gets its energy from the sun. Follow the arrows to show the animal that eats the plant. Then, the animal that eats that animal. What eats that animal? Draw it in the next circle. Use the animals illustrated.

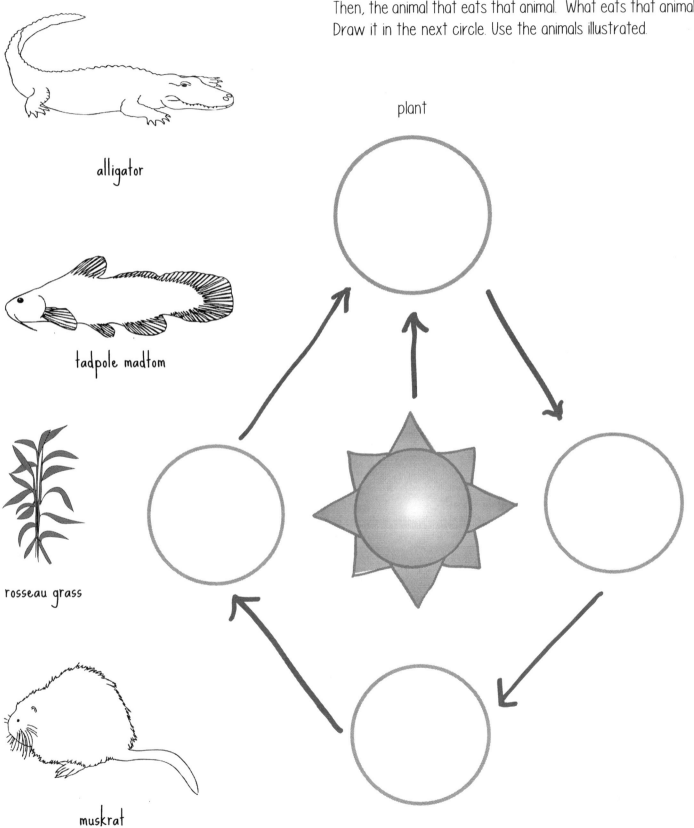

alligator

tadpole madtom

rosseau grass

muskrat

plant

Animal Research

Choose an animal of the Wetlands of North America.
You can pick from your animals cards if you like. Draw and write about this animal.

Animal name   Class   Biome

_____   _____   _____

_____

_____

_____

_____

How Do They Interact?

Muskrats and Rosseau grass live in the Wetlands in the Mississippi Delta region. Draw their pictures in the boxes where they belong. Write their names underneath.

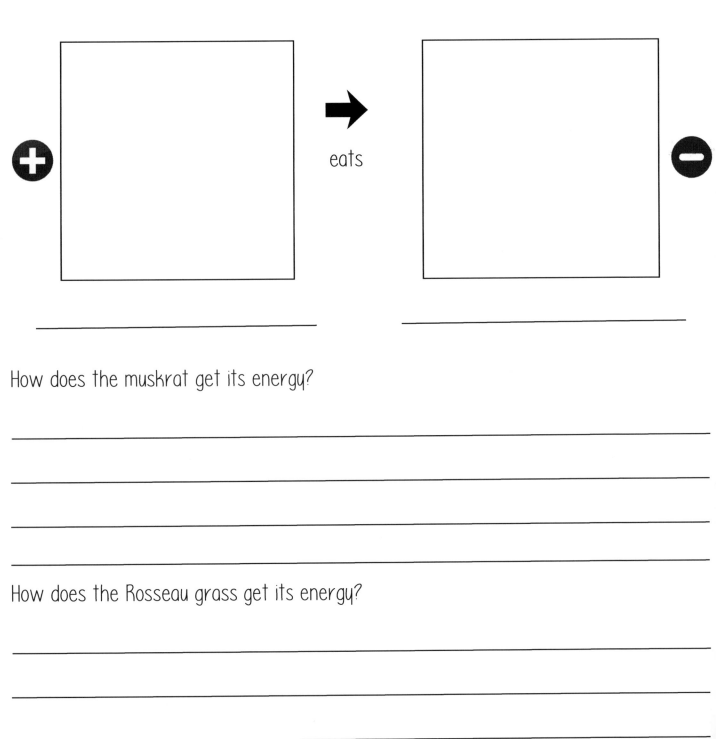

➕   ➡️ eats   ➖

_____   _____

How does the muskrat get its energy?

_____

_____

_____

How does the Rosseau grass get its energy?

_____

_____

_____

Plant Research

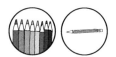

Choose a plant of the Wetlands of North America.
You can pick from your cards if you like. Draw and write about this plant.

Plant name   Class   Biome

_____   _____   _____

_____

_____

_____

_____

Things I know now about the Wetlands of North America

_____

_____

_____

_____

_____

_____

Things I wonder about the Wetlands of North America

_____

_____

_____

_____

_____

_____

From Louisiana to Panama!

Achutupu, Panama

Use different shades of green to color in the Tropical Forest.

The Tropical Forest

An isthmus is a narrow strip of land connecting two larger land areas, usually with water on either side. The southern isthmus that connects North America to South America is almost all tropical forest. There are many layers of the forest. Each layer provides a different kind of habitat.

Sailing Tour of Achutupu

You and your mom have flown from Panama City to a tiny airport on the mainland of Panama. You are going to visit a girl named Otilda, who lives on the island of Achutupu. It is very hot in Panama! When you get off the plane, walk north from the small building at the airport to the dock. You see Otilda, her pet pig and her uncle waiting by a dugout canoe, called a cayuca. It is made by carving out a tree trunk. "Nuweigambi," she says with a smile. "Nice to meet you," she says in very good English. You are happy she speaks English, because your Guna is not so good. You sail across the bay to the dock on the south side of Achutupu. On the way, Otilda tells you a little about her little island. There are no cars, no electricity and no fresh water. The island is where the houses are, but all of the food is grown on the mainland near the river. Everyone in Achutupu lives with their families. Otilda lives with her grandparents, her parents, two aunts, two uncles and 9 cousins. She laughs at your look of disbelief. "Don't worry, you will stay at the hotel!" she says.

HOW TO USE THE MAP: Trace where you went on your visit with Otilda. Start and end at the airport.

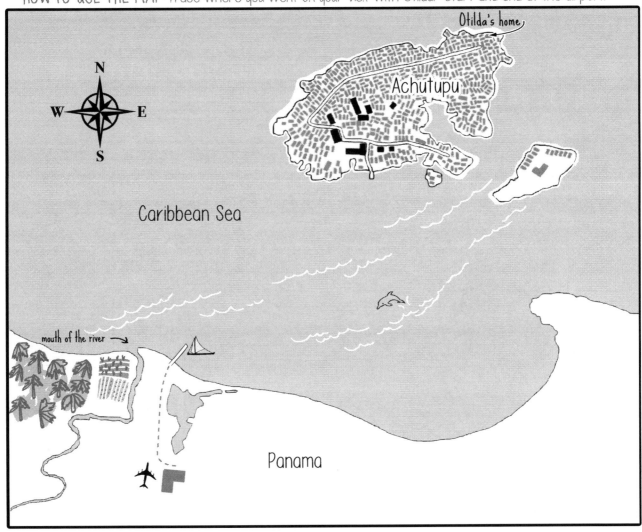

It is not long before you dock at Achutupu. You follow Otilda and her pet pig into the village. You come to a large building on the left and take the path west. People and children are busy everywhere. Children are running around laughing and playing. You follow the path all the way to the northeast corner of the island. You come to Otilda's house. It is next to the beach. You meet her family. They are very nice. You share a dinner of rice, plantains and fish. After dinner, everyone walks to the beach, where the water is clear and blue. On the beach, there is another cayuca. Otilda and her Dad take you and your mom to a hotel on a smaller island southeast of Achutupu, where you and your Mom will stay. The hotel is owned by a Guna family. You get to pick out the hut you will stay in. There are hammocks instead of beds.

Dolphin in Caribbean Sea!

The next morning, Otilda comes to the hotel to pick up you and your Mom in a cayuca. This time she is with her grandmother, mother and aunts who are going to the river on the mainland to bathe, wash clothes and get water to take back to the island. They sit in the boat in a special order with grandmother at the stern. Your mom smiles at you, and you know she is thinking that it is a special experience to spend the day with this family of women. You sit with Otilda at the bow and sail southwest towards the mouth of the river on the shores of Panama.

A dolphin swims alongside the cayuca! Otilda tells you about how her uncle asked the dolphin for a baby girl and the dolphin brought her to him. Otilda looks back at her cousin and says, "Is this the same dolphin that brought you to us? It must be seeing if you are well."

You dock the boat on the beach by the mouth of the river. You and Otilda go for a walk in the tropical forest while the women talk and wash clothes in the river. It is cooler and noisy in the forest. Birds are calling to one another. Otilda sees a tree frog and puts him on her finger to show you. You hear a rustle nearby on the ground. You both peek between the branches to see a bird with black feathers and a yellow beak. It has a fan of curled feathers on its head. Otilda knows the names of all of the animals, but they are in her own language.

Tiny tree frog

Back at the river, the clothes are drying in the sun. The women are working on their molas. Otilda is learning to sew and shows you the monkey on the mola she is making. She tells you a story about a monkey that was throwing nuts at her one day when she went to the river. She gives you a mola that she made with a dolphin on it. You tell her that you will keep it always. Too soon, the sun gets lower in the sky. Your mom tells you it is time to catch the plane that will take you back to the bigger airport. You go back to the beach, from here you will take the cayuca the short distance back to the dock at the airport. Otilda and the women say, "Takeimalo," and you know that it must mean goodbye. You hug Otilda and thank her and her family. What an amazing trip this has been!

Design a Mola

Molas are created by artists using fabrics in many vibrant colors. Often finished molas are then sewn onto blouses to make wearable art!

NOTES:

Take some time to color design Otilda's monkey mola. It is made of simple shapes with thick black outlines. What else do you notice? Think about the elements of this art style and take notes. Create a mola design of your own following some of these notes. You could use any artist supply that will show up on this black rectangle. Chalk or colored pencils may work best!

Medicinal Plants

An extract of this plant's seeds can be given in small sips for treatment of snake bites, and scorpion, centipede and other poisonous stings. Many herbalists prefer this plant to others for its multiple uses. Its grated seeds are also used for stomach pain, and an extract of the bark can be made into a lotion to treat body aches.

Ina gabid
Simaba Cedron Planch

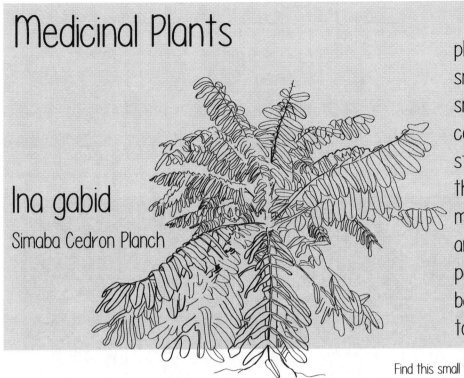

Find this small tree at the edge of the forest and color it blue

Abior
Dieffenbachia pittieri

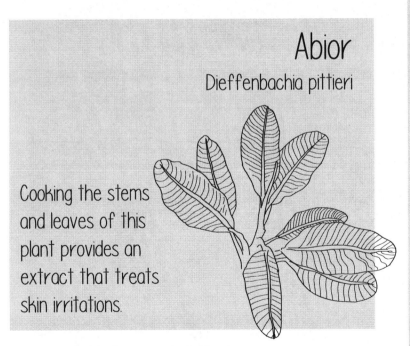

Cooking the stems and leaves of this plant provides an extract that treats skin irritations.

Find this plant by the river and color it red.

Esnargan
Acrostichum aureum

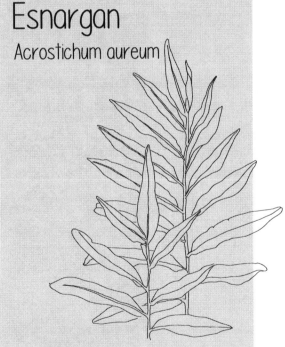

A medicinal bath is made to care for dizzy spells or headaches. A paste is made from the leaves and placed in the nostrils of infants to treat colds.

Find this fern by the river and color it yellow.

Find the medicinal plants in this scene.
What other useful plants might you find here?

Leaf Cutter Ants Grow Food

A new queen is born in a leaf cutter nest. She is larger than the other young ants. Most of the larvae are female workers. A few of them are males or drones. The gardener ants bring the newly hatched ants fungus to eat. As soon as the workers, gardeners and soldiers are big enough, they begin their work for the colony. The drones will eat and lay around until they are old enough to mate with the queen. The queen and the drones are the only ants with wings. One day, the queen takes some of the mushroom food from the gardener ants and tucks it into a pocket in her head. Then she flies up out of the nest. One of the drones follows her. They touch and mate. The drone falls down and soon dies.

The queen goes off to find her new nest. She finds some bare ground and begins to dig. She digs until she is safely in the ground. Then she begins to lay thousands and thousands of eggs every day! Some of the larvae grow to be gardener ants. One of their jobs is to take care of the queen and the newly hatched larvae. The gardener ants start feeding the larvae with the fungus the queen brought from the old nest. Some of the ants grow up to be workers and soldiers. They leave the nest to go in search of leaves. They go off in a line, leaving a scent trail so that they can find their way back to the nest. They are looking for special leaves. They check out some leaves, but they are not the right ones. Finally, they find the right leaves. The soldiers keep a lookout while the workers begin to use their scissor-like jaws to cut the leaves. They cut pieces two or three times their own weight. They eat the sap from the leaves for energy. When all of the workers have a leaf to carry, they begin the journey back to the nest. They follow one behind the other. The soldiers are looking out for the giant bala ant. "Bala" means "bullet" in Spanish. He has a bite that is deadly like a bullet. They make it safely back to the nest, where they give the leaves to the gardener ants. The gardener ants take them and lick them clean. Then they cut them into smaller pieces and chew them up. They add these chewed up leaves to the garden. Fungus grows on the chewed up leaves. The ants take the fungus to the larvae to eat before it sprouts into a mushroom. They tend the fungus and do not let any other kinds of fungus grow in the garden. The ants are like farmers who grow their food. The ants take care of the fungus, and the fungus takes care of the ants.

Why do you think the worker ants walk in a line one behind the other?

_____

_____

How does the fungus get the energy it needs to grow?

_____

_____

Imagine that you are one of the ants in the story. You might be the queen, a drone, a gardener, a worker or a soldier. Imagine that you are that ant and tell the story as the ant you have chosen. What happened to you?

_____

_____

_____

_____

_____

_____

_____

_____

_____

_____

_____

_____

_____

_____

_____

_____

_____

_____

How Do They Interact?

Leafcutter ants "farm" a special fungus to feed themselves in the Tropical Forest of North America. The fungus and the ants help one another. The way they interact is called symbiosis. Draw their pictures in the correct boxes.

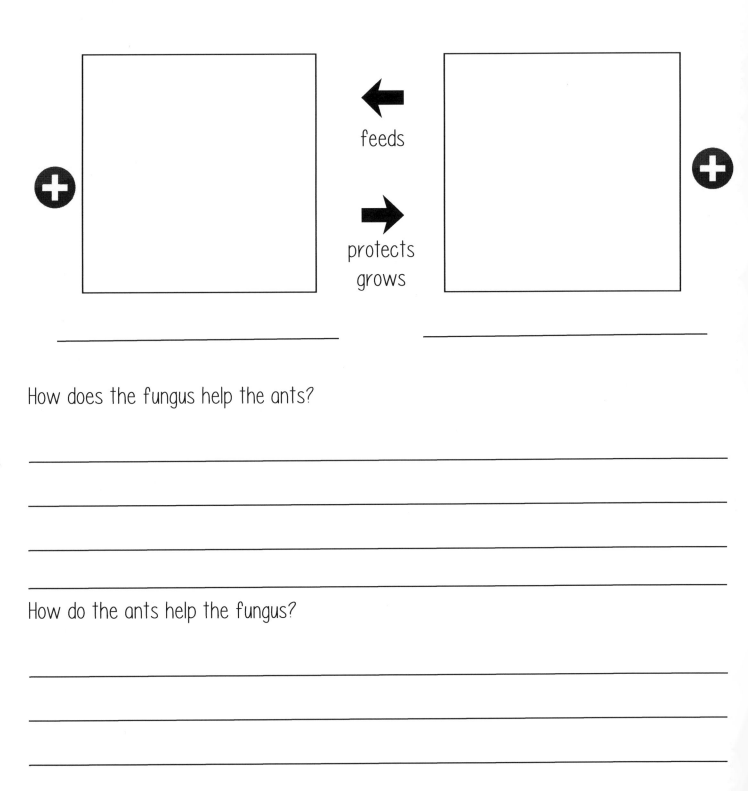

feeds

protects
grows

How does the fungus help the ants?

_____

_____

_____

How do the ants help the fungus?

_____

_____

_____

Parts of a Leaf-Cutter Ant Hill

Study this ant hill and the members of its colony.
Then put them to work by drawing them in their stations!

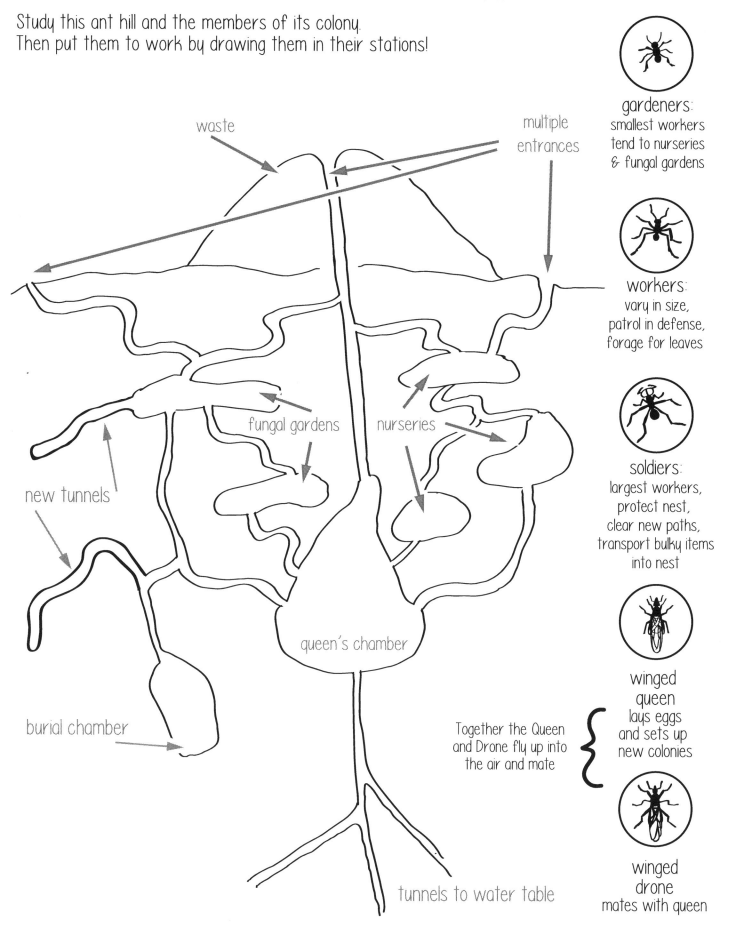

waste

multiple entrances

gardeners: smallest workers tend to nurseries & fungal gardens

workers: vary in size, patrol in defense, forage for leaves

new tunnels

fungal gardens

nurseries

soldiers: largest workers, protect nest, clear new paths, transport bulky items into nest

queen's chamber

burial chamber

Together the Queen and Drone fly up into the air and mate

winged queen lays eggs and sets up new colonies

winged drone mates with queen

tunnels to water table

Draw a currasow in the Tropical Forest biome.

Use a pencil to draw the gray lines. Draw the black lines with a pen. Then erase the pencil lines.

He looks for food on the forest floor. Finish drawing the forest behind and around the currasow. Color the currasow by looking at the card and noticing its markings.

Parts of a Flower

Study the parts of a tropical fuschia flower. Then draw your own flower and label its parts. It can be a real flower or one you create from your imagination.

A sepal is part of the calyx.

The calyx is comprised of its sepals.

The corolla is the formation of petals within the sepals enclosing the reproductive organs.

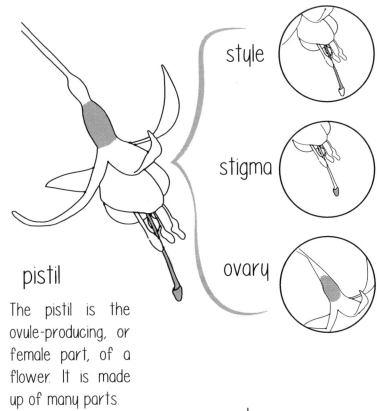

style

stigma

ovary

pistil

The pistil is the ovule-producing, or female part, of a flower. It is made up of many parts.

stamen

The stamen is the pollen producing, or male part, of a flower. It has two parts.

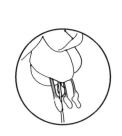

anther

filament

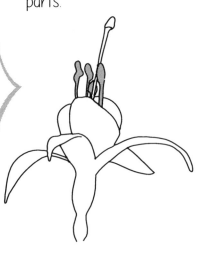

Design your own flower. Keep in mind the many parts a flower needs to reproduce.

Animal Research

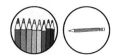

Choose an animal of the Tropical Forest of North America.
You can pick from your animals cards if you like. Draw and write about this animal.

Animal name   *Class*   *Biome*

_____   _____   _____

_____

_____

_____

_____

Tropical Forest Food Chain

Start by drawing or writing the banana tree in the top circle for the plant that gets its energy from the sun. Follow the arrows to show the animal that eats the plant. Then, the animal that eats that animal. What eats that animal? Draw or write it in the next circle. Use the animals illustrated.

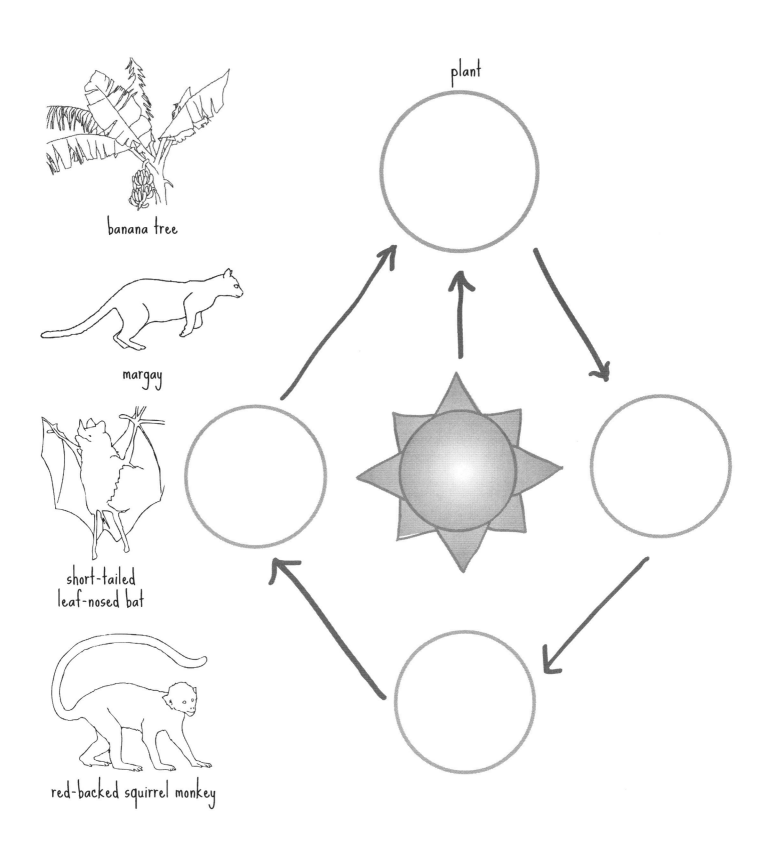

banana tree

margay

short-tailed
leaf-nosed bat

red-backed squirrel monkey

plant

Adaptation Matching

The Tropical Forest is crowded and full of life. Draw a line from the animal to the description of how it lives in its biome. Write a description of how the potto has adapted to life in the Tropical Forest..

hog-nosed viper

This animal has a bright red color that warns other animals that it has poisonous skin. The mother takes her tadpoles to flowers that fill up with water from the day's rain.

strawberry poison-dart frog

This reptile looks just like the forest floor where it lives. It hides among the leaves and waits for prey to come by.

royal flycatcher

This animal eats insects. It builds its nest in branches that hang over water. The female is brown to blend in with the forest. The male has a red comb to get attention from the female.

potto

_____

_____

_____

_____

Animal Research

Choose an animal of the Tropical Forest of North America.
You can pick from your animals cards if you like. Draw and write about this animal.

Animal name

Class

Biome

_____

_____

_____

_____

_____

_____

_____

Things I know now about the Tropical Forest of North America

_____

_____

_____

_____

_____

_____

Things I wonder about the Tropical Forest of North America

_____

_____

_____

_____

_____

_____

Let's go from Panama to Arizona!

Shonto, Arizona

The Desert

The desert is a land that is very dry and very hot during the day. It can be very cold at night. It rains very little, but when it does, there can be a flood. In the southwest, there are canyons cut by rivers. The land is rocky.

An Exciting Visit with Shándíín

Travel northeast by car on Hwy 163 until you see the sign for Monument Valley Navajo Tribal Park. Look around at all of the amazing orange and red rock formations. It is beautiful in the early morning light. Shándíín is waiting for you outside. She greets you and takes you to an exhibit in the visitor's center that explains how Monument Valley was formed.

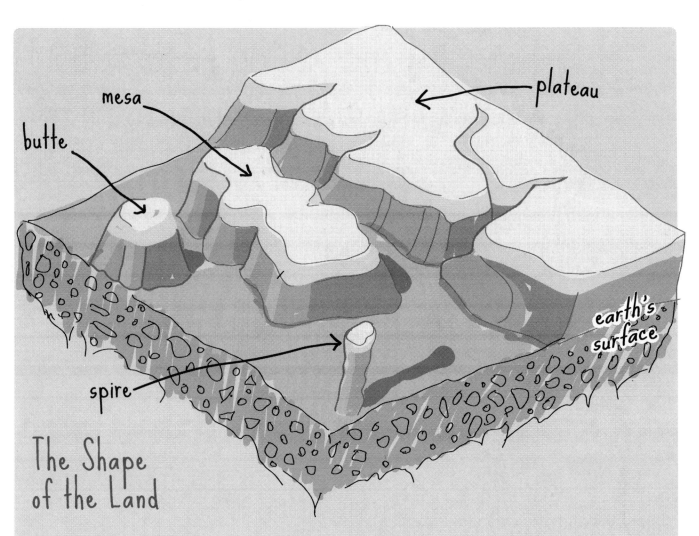

The Shape of the Land

The earth's surface continues its constant evolution as it is exposed to wind and water. These two elements pass over landforms, taking pieces of earth with them as they move. This is erosion. Sandstone is easily eroded, and the wind, rain and cycles of frost and heat have been at work for over 50 million years, cracking and sculpting the valley to its present form.

In the arid climate of the desert, the beauty of ancient landforms stands out in a landscape of minimal vegetation. There are many different types of landforms created by erosion. Plateaus are large expanses of land that rise high above its surroundings and have at least one steep side. Mesas look just like a mountain with a flat top. A mesa is an isolated plateau. Buttes are a smaller version of a mesa. They can be eroded more to become spire monuments or pinnacles. In Monument Valley, you will see how erosion has worked to create a place the Diné have found to be sacred.

The Anasazi Ruins and the Art of the Petroglyph

Petroglyphs are rock carvings made by pecking directly on the rock surface, using a stone chisel and a hammerstone. When the surface of the rock was chipped off, the lighter rock underneath was exposed, creating the petroglyph. These carvings appear all over the world. They were used by ancient people to tell a story or to mark a spot. They were also used to show the presence of game, shelter and water. Other symbols such as zigzags, spirals, dots and circles within circles may show the movements of planets in the night sky.

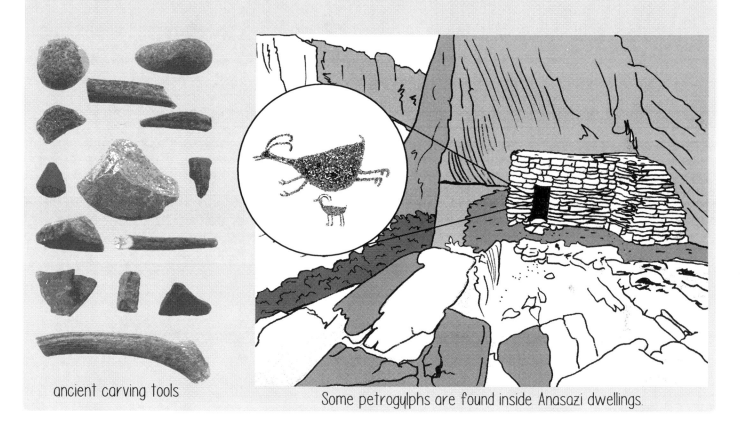

ancient carving tools

Some petroglyphs are found inside Anasazi dwellings.

Hit the Trail!

As you come out of the visitor's center, you see the famous Mittens and Merrick Butte. Shándíín says that the Mittens are also known to the Diné as the "hands of God." Shándíín's Uncle Albert is ready to take you on a tour of the park. He calls this place Tsé Bii' Ndzisgaii, which means "valley of the rocks." They will take you to some places that you can only go to with a member of the tribe. He has some horses tied up nearby. Shándíín introduces you to a pony named Spirit. She says that he is very easy going and will follow the other horses. Shándíín's uncle gives you a lift up. Spirit stands still until the other horses set off at a slow walk. He follows behind. You are heading southeast, away from the visitor's center.

Turn the page to go on a trail ride with Shándíín and her uncle Albert.

Monument Valley on Horseback

Begin the ride by heading southeast, away from the visitor's center. The horses follow a path between Elephant Butte and Camel Butte. Next, you come to a round hole in the rock called Window. From here you keep riding south, passing Spearhead mesa to the east.

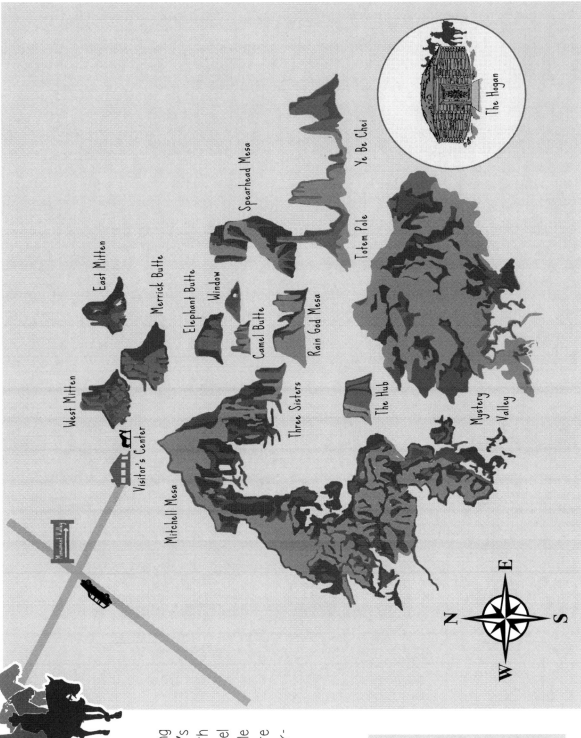

West Mitten

East Mitten

Merrick Butte

Elephant Butte

Window

Camel Butte

Rain God Mesa

Spearhead Mesa

Totem Pole

Ye Be Chei

The Hogan

Three Sisters

The Hub

Mystery Valley

Mitchell Mesa

Visitor's Center

Monument Valley

N E W S

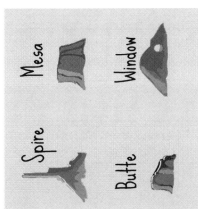

Spire

Mesa

Butte

Window

HAPPY TRAILS: Read the story and use this map to imagine your trail ride through the many rock formations of Monument Valley.

VISIT THE HOGAN:

You come out of the valley and see a spire that's called "Totem Pole." The tower behind it is called "Ye Be Chei" in the language of the Diné; it means "ceremonial dancer." You head east towards the second spire.

"Look! See the dancers coming out of a hogan?" he asks.

Yes, you can see one standing tall and one hunched over his drum. Albert tells you how the medicine men used hogans, a house made of wood and earth, for ceremonies. He asks if you would like to visit a hogan. You nod eagerly. You head southeast away from Ye Be Chei. Soon, you see a dome-shaped building and some sheep being driven by a boy on horseback. He waves as you come closer to the hogan. An older woman comes out. She is wearing a long skirt, beautiful turquoise jewelry and tennis shoes! She invites you to come inside and see the rug she is weaving. You sit on the cool earthen floor and watch her work. Her hands move with a rhythm across the loom. Before you leave, she gives you a small leather pouch. Inside is a turquoise stone, a piece of wool dyed yellow and a red rock. She suggests that you be on the lookout for something to add to it to remember your trip.

ANCIENT ANASAZI:

You wave goodbye and head north back toward Totem Pole. Shándíín points out the Hub up ahead. This small mesa sits at the entrance to Mystery Valley. Shándíín tells you that Mystery Valley was the home of the Anasazi, a people who lived here long before the Diné came. When you get to the Hub, you turn the horses south. As you ride through the valley you see petroglyphs, drawings made by the Anasazi. The picture is of bighorn sheep. You ask if the bighorn sheep still live here. Albert answers, "Not for hundreds of years." You think that there must have been more water in this place when the Anasazi lived here. It is getting later in the day, and the mesa makes a cool shadow. You see that there are wide caves in the side of the mesa. Shándíín points to one and dismounts from her horse. You tie Spirit to a small juniper and climb up the side of the mesa after her. You come to the edge of the arched opening. Against the back wall is a very small stone house. "This is where the ancient ones lived," whispers Shándíín. There are bits of pottery on the ground. You think about taking a piece of pottery for your pouch, but it seems wrong to disturb this place. You sit with Shándíín and share some fry bread and water. You look out over Mystery Valley and wonder what it would have been like to live here.

WHAT'S IN A NAME?:

As you climb back down the mesa, you notice that the shadows have grown even longer across the floor of the valley. With Albert's help, you climb back on Spirit and follow the other horses north out of the valley. You take the path around the east side of The Hub. Shándíín rides beside you and tells you that the rocks you see in front of you are called Rain God Mesa. It was named for the rain god, who stored water for the people. You see dark streaks that show where water comes out of the ground at the base of the mesa. Up ahead on the left, you see three more spires. Shándíín asks, "What do they look like to you?" You squint your eyes and say "A mother, father and child in the middle!" Shándíín laughs and says, "You are close. We call it the Three Sisters. That is the younger one in the middle."

Your path takes you north, past the Camel Butte to the east and back to the visitor's center. You get down from the pony, a bit sore from the ride. You look to the ground and see a tiny feather. It is just the right size for your pouch! You show it to Shándíín and her uncle. You hear a high pitched tweet behind you and see a small brown bird hopping about on the rocks. Shándíín says, "He says you are very welcome!" The sun is setting on the red rocks of Monument Valley as you say goodbye to your new friends.

A Day in the Life of Shándiín

Use the word bank to finish this story about
a typical day in the desert

hogan	turquoise	weave	reservation	serape	Diné Bizaad
sheep	tell stories	fry bread	truck	mutton stew	barrel racing

Yá'át'ééh! My family wakes up early to go for a run. We run towards

the rising sun to receive its energy and set our intentions for the day.

When we get back, I wash up for school. My family lives in a house, but we also

have a _____ on our land for ceremonies.

To get ready for school, I take a shower, but many families on the

_____ live without running water

and must bathe with a bowl of water and a towel.

I get dressed and put on my favorite

_____ bracelet

for good luck—I have a math test at school today!

My brothers and I feed the horses, _____,

and dogs, and my mother prepares breakfast for the family. We eat

_____ or porridge,

and my parents and brothers drink coffee with lots of sugar.

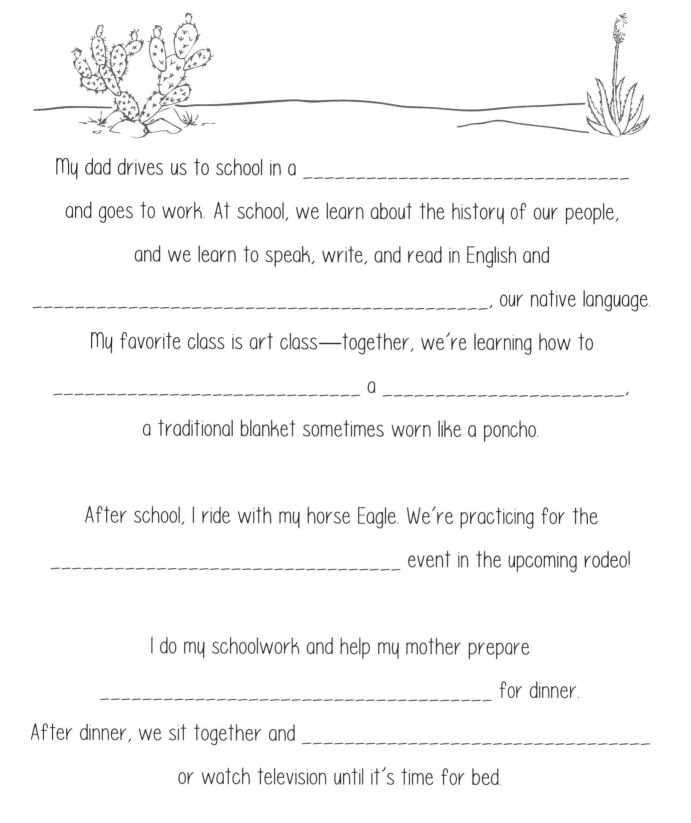

My dad drives us to school in a _____

and goes to work. At school, we learn about the history of our people,

and we learn to speak, write, and read in English and

_____, our native language.

My favorite class is art class—together, we're learning how to

_____ a _____,

a traditional blanket sometimes worn like a poncho.

After school, I ride with my horse Eagle. We're practicing for the

_____ event in the upcoming rodeo!

I do my schoolwork and help my mother prepare

_____ for dinner.

After dinner, we sit together and _____

or watch television until it's time for bed.

Yá'át'ééh hiiłchi'į'

 # Weaving a Story

Serapes, or Dine tapestries, are commonly found in many homes across North America. They are used as decorative floor coverings, blankets and wall hangings. They also make great saddle blankets, cloaks and dresses. Weavers use many geometric shapes and symbols to bring stories and meaning to their work. They design the serapes to be symmetrical when complete. This means that the same design is found on the left and the right. Traditional colors would have been browns, whites, grays and a little indigo blue. Red would be a rare and difficult color to find in nature. Synthetic fibers are now available in many colors!

Design the colors of this serape however you like!

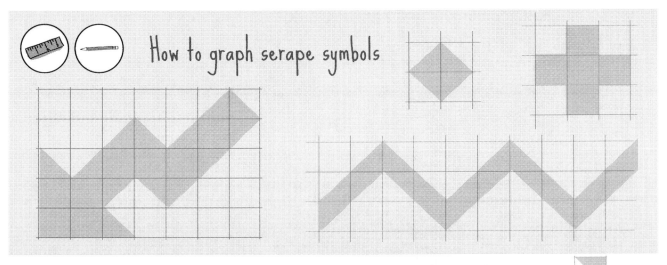

Notice how some designs are made with diagonal lines across the square.

Now you can design a weaving that would use colors, shapes and symmetry to tell a story or represent an idea

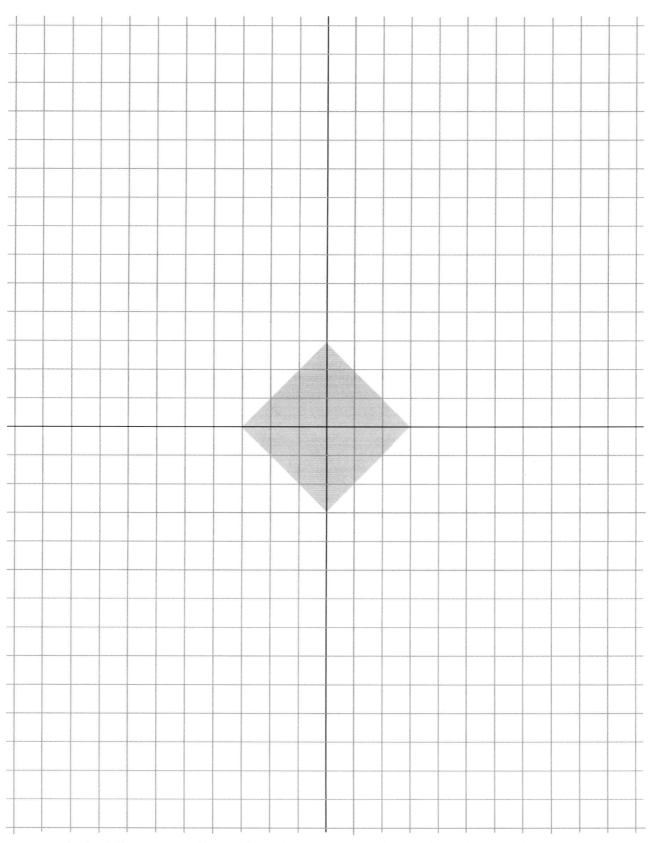

Look at the square in the middle— the design is made by a diagonal across the squares

The Hogan

The Diné used to live in hogans. These are structures made of timber or stone, and packed with earth with the door facing to the east to welcome the rising sun. Finish this drawing here and on the next page. What plants and animals might be living around this hogan?

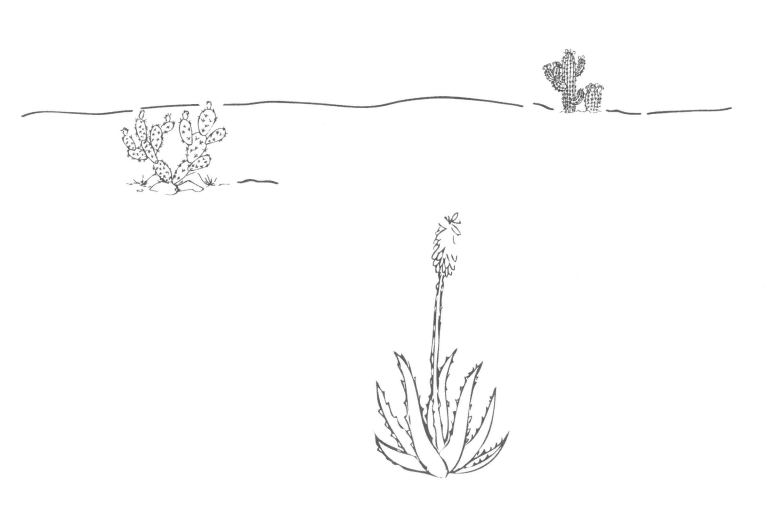

Day and Night in the Desert

It is early morning in the desert. It is just starting to warm up from the chill of the night. A chuckwalla comes out onto a rock to warm up. He is moving slow. The roadrunner's body has been chilled during the night, too. It spreads its wings and raises its feathers so that the sun hits the patches of black skin on its back. When it warms up, the roadrunner goes hunting for breakfast. It spots the chuckwalla on the rock and darts quickly to grab it in its beak before it can move away. But the chuckwalla has warmed up, too, and it goes quickly into a crack in the rocks. It takes a deep breath and wedges itself in the rock as it holds in the air. The roadrunner tries to pull the chuckwalla from the rocks, but it is stuck tight. The roadrunner speeds away to find an easier meal. A desert tortoise comes out of its burrow. Its shell protects it from the sun, which is getting warmer and warmer. This female is going to lay her eggs. She digs a hole with her claws and deposits the eggs there. She covers them up and leaves to look for something to eat. The eggs will hatch later, and the babies will be on their own. The tortoise finds the fruit of a prickly pear cactus. She has no teeth to bite the fruit but uses her beak. This food is close to the nest. Maybe the babies will find it, too.

The sun is high and very hot now. Nothing is stirring in the desert. The jackrabbit has dug a shallow pit under a bush. It is very still. The rattlesnake is in its burrow. The kangaroo rat is in his burrow munching seeds that he collected last night. The tiny bit of water in the seeds is all the water the kangaroo rat needs. The kit fox is in her den with her pups. They are still drinking her milk, but after ten weeks, they are ready for meat. Later, she will come out to hunt for them. Finally, the hot desert sun reaches the horizon, where the earth and sky meet. Slowly it sinks down in a flaming orange sunset.

Almost at once, the air begins to cool. The diamond-backed rattlesnake comes out from his hole and flicks out his tongue to test the air. The kangaroo rat comes scurrying near, looking for seeds to stuff in his cheek pouches. The rattler senses the rat's body heat with his tongue. He strikes and sinks his fangs into the rat. His venom kills his prey instantly, and he unhinges his jaws to swallow the kangaroo rat whole.

The kit fox comes out of her den, searching for mice or ground squirrels to feed her pups. She sniffs the night air and perks her ears to hear a rustle in the bushes. She hears the jackrabbit hop quietly over to a cactus, biting into it for a drink of water. She creeps almost silently but the jackrabbit with its huge ears hears and jumps quickly out of range. The jackrabbit is too large a prey for the kit fox, anyway, and she turns away when she realizes who made the rustling sound. She is only as big as a house cat herself and must find smaller prey. The kit fox hunts without luck through the night. Just as dawn starts to come up over the horizon, she spots a scorpion making his way back to his hole. She pounces and takes her prize quickly back to her den and the pups who are waiting for her return. A new day in the desert is about to begin.

What is the hottest part of the day in the desert?

_____

Why does the rattler need to sense body heat to hunt?

_____

_____

Adaptation Matching

The desert is hot and dry, but cool at night. Draw a line from the animal to the description of how it lives in its biome. What does the tortoise have to help him dig a burrow so that it can stay cool?

mule deer

It can burrow into the ground to wait for rain so that it can lay its eggs in a puddle. The tadpoles can grow fast before the puddle dries.

antelope jackrabbit

This animal can smell underground water. Then it digs down with its large hooves to find the water. It can dig holes two feet deep.

toad

It has big ears to hear sounds at night that will keep it safe from other animals that would eat it. Its ears help it to lose heat fast by bringing its blood close to its skin.

desert tortoise

_____

_____

_____

_____

Draw an Antelope Jackrabbit in his Desert biome.

Use a pencil to draw the gray lines. Draw the black lines with a pen. Then erase the pencil lines.

After you draw the jackrabbit, draw some more cactus in his biome.
A mesa is a mountain with a flat top. Draw one on the horizon.

Parts of a Gila {HEE-luh} Monster

Fill in the diagram. Then write about its adaptations.

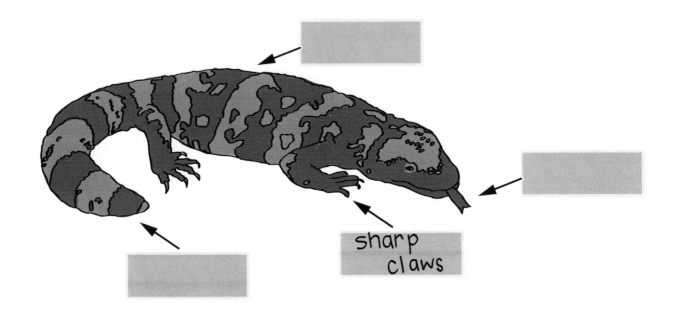

sharp
claws

sharp claws   fat storage   camouflage   forked tongue

It has sharp claws to dig burrows.

Animal Research

Choose an animal from the Desert of North America.
You can pick from your animals cards if you like.
Draw and write about this animal.

Animal name

Class

Biome

Plant Research

Choose a plant from the Desert of North America.
You can pick from your cards if you like. Draw and write about this plant.

Plant name

Class

Biome

_____ _____ _____

_____

_____

_____

_____

Parts of a Cactus

Read about the adaptations of a cactus. Use this information to fill in the diagram.

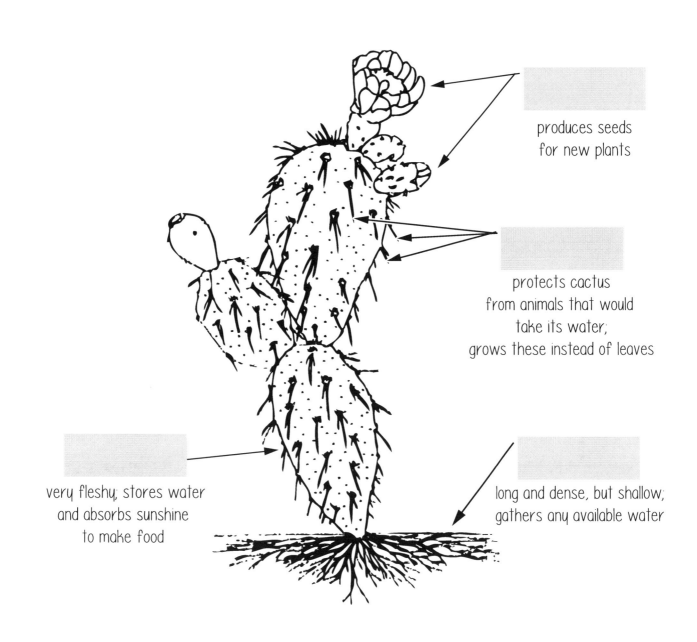

produces seeds
for new plants

protects cactus
from animals that would
take its water;
grows these instead of leaves

very fleshy; stores water
and absorbs sunshine
to make food

long and dense, but shallow;
gathers any available water

stem   roots   spines   flower

How Do They Interact?

Find two animals in the Desert of North America. One should be a predator and the other should be its prey. Draw them in the box where they belong and write their names underneath.

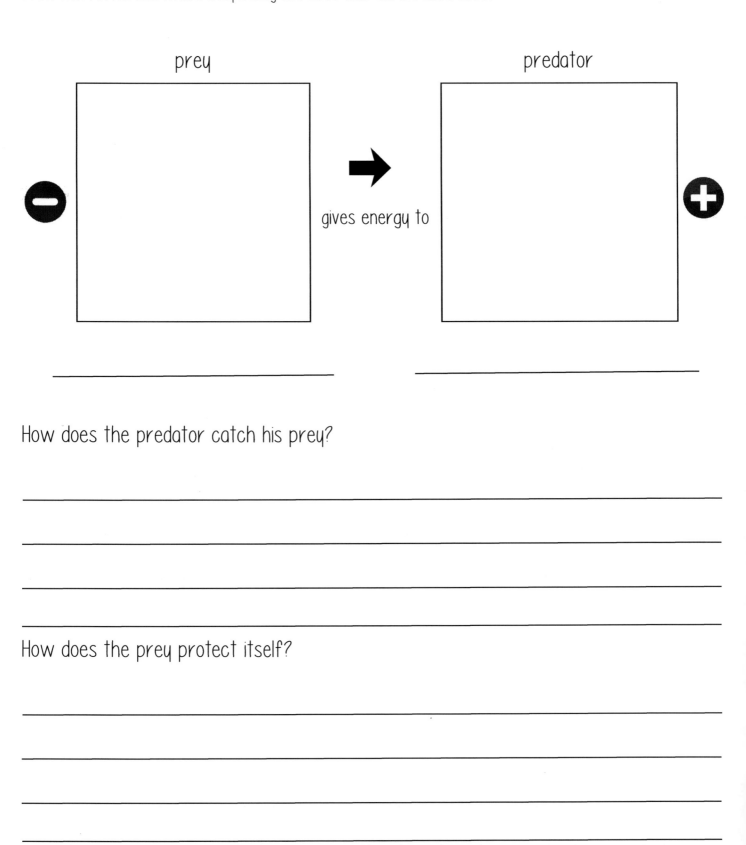

prey   predator

gives energy to

_____   _____

How does the predator catch his prey?

_____

_____

_____

How does the prey protect itself?

_____

_____

_____

Animal Research

Choose an animal from the Desert of North America.
You can pick from your animals cards if you like.
Draw and write about this animal.

Animal name

Class

Biome

Desert Food Chain

Start by drawing or writing the name of the ocotillo in the top circle for the plant that gets its energy from the sun. Follow the arrows to show the animal that eats the seeds of the ocotillo. Then, the animal that eats that animal. What eats the animal that eats the animal? Draw or write its name in the next circle. Use the animals illustrated.

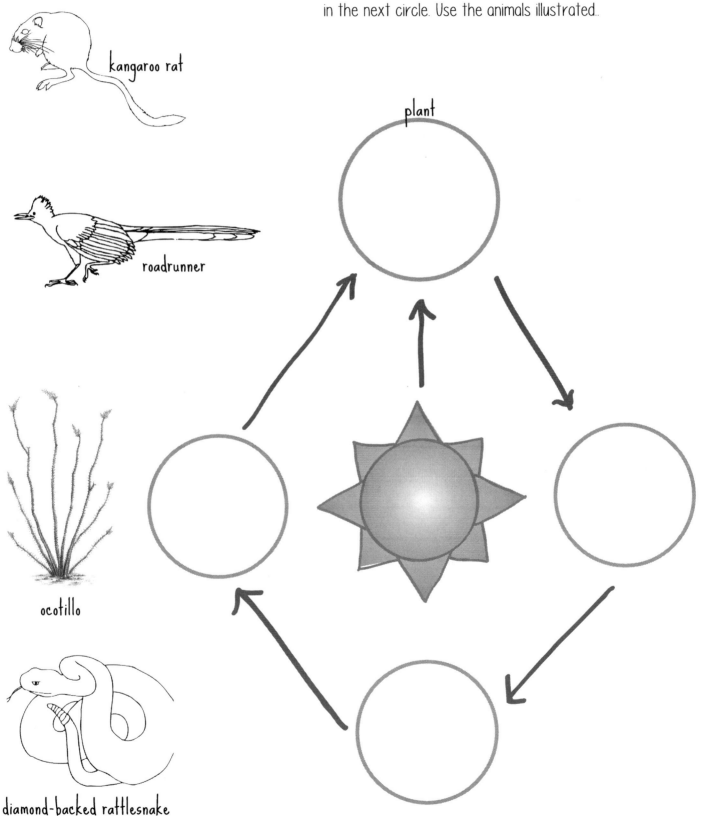

kangaroo rat

roadrunner

ocotillo

diamond-backed rattlesnake

plant

Plant Research

Choose a plant from the Desert of North America.
You can pick from your cards if you like. Draw and write about this plant.

Plant name   Class   Biome

_____   _____   _____

_____

_____

_____

_____

Things I know now about the Desert of North America

_____

_____

_____

_____

_____

_____

Things I wonder about the Desert of North America

_____

_____

_____

_____

_____

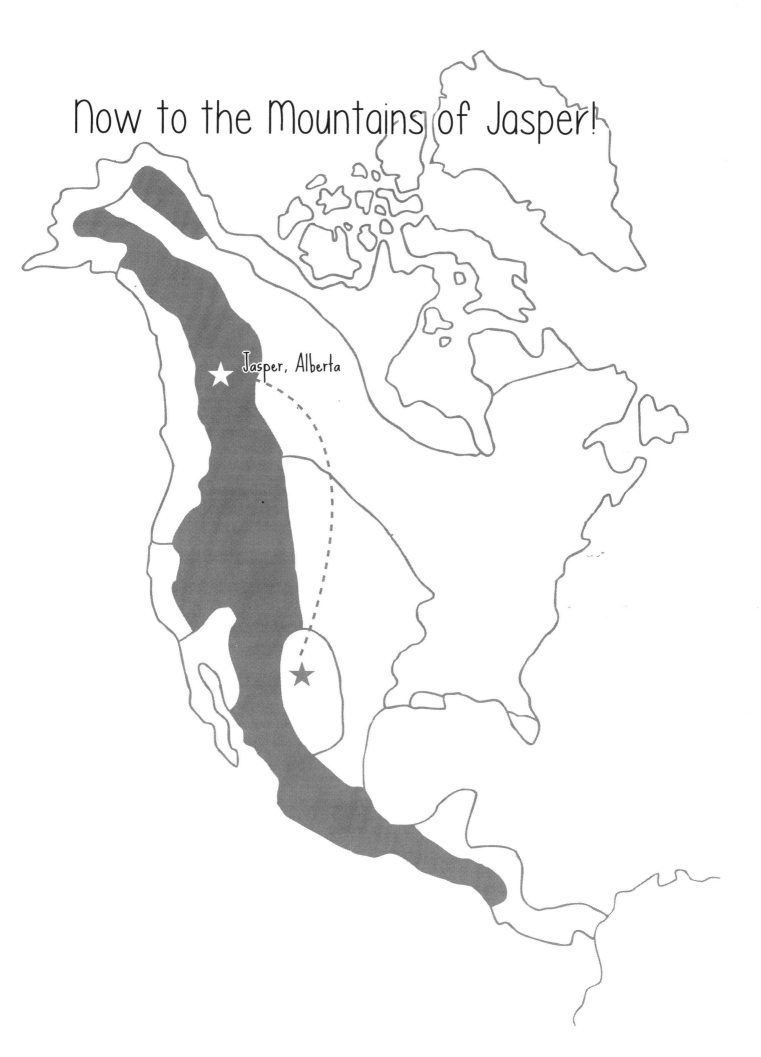

Now to the Mountains of Jasper!

Jasper, Alberta

The Mountains

This biome is home to many different kinds of plants and animals. Three different conditions that affect the type of life found on a mountain are latitude, altitude and rainfall. The Mountains we will now explore are far away from the equator and vary in their height and weather. We will find much diversity in a cold mountain climate.

Amazing Jasper National Park

You've flown into Prince George today to visit your friend Logan. You drive east on the Highway 16 into Jasper with your family. You are staying just outside of town in a cabin. You haven't seen Logan since he moved to Jasper a year ago. You meet Logan and his mom in town. She's a park ranger at Jasper National Park and his dad is a wildlife biologist.

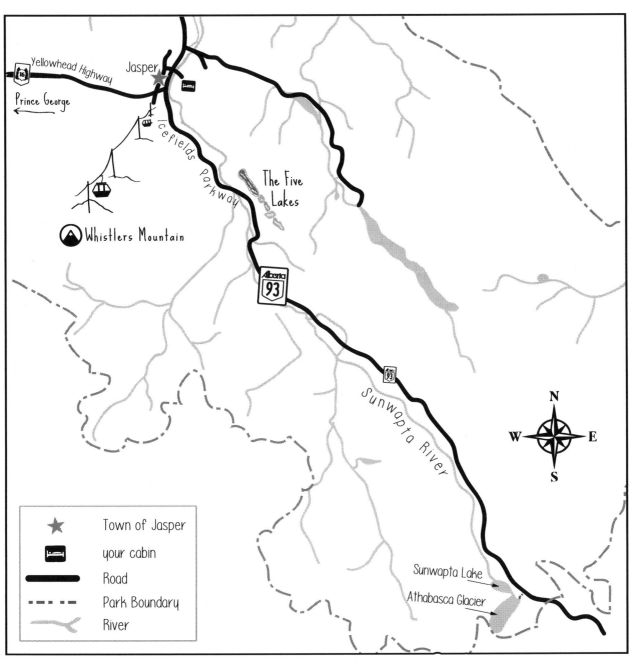

Read the story on the next page and trace the course you took on the map

aerial lift

DAY 1: Logan suggests that you take the aerial lift to the top of Whistler Mountain to see as much of the park as you can from one place. You walk south from town and cross over the Yellowhead Hwy. You walk down a road to the place where you get on the lift. You look out the windows as the town of Jasper gets smaller. The tops of the mountains are rocky with patches of snow, even in August! Logan tells you that the mountain is named after the marmots that live there. They whistle to one another to signal danger. When you get off the lift, you are 7,500 ft high. Logan shows you a trail that will take you to the top of the mountain.

Soon, you will see an outcropping of rock with furry little animals popping in and out of little caves in the rock. It's the marmots! They are warming themselves in the sun and do not seem disturbed by your presence. When you get to the very top, you see the Five Lakes to the southeast. Logan points out an eagle soaring in the distance. You take the lift back down and take Logan to show him your cabin so that he can come and get you in the morning. You take a swim in the river near your cabin. The water is really cold! When you get back to the cabin, Logan calls and says that he and his mom will pick you up in the morning to do something really cool!

DAY 2: In the morning, Logan and his mom pick you up at your cabin and you drive south out of Jasper on the Icefields Parkway. You are surrounded by an incredible landscape. You see a sign for Five Lakes Trail. Stop here and take a short hike to a beautiful little lake. It's called the Fifth Lake. You can guess what the next one is named but you are surprised that it is a different color blue. Logan says that it is the rock sediment in the water that causes this special effect. Third and Second Lakes are different, too. You go around First Lake and head back for the jeep. "That was pretty cool," you say. "That's not even the coolest thing, though," says Logan.

You travel further south down the Icefields Highway, past snow hanging on the sides of mountains and high valleys. Finally, you come to a sign that reads: Athabasca Glacier. You take a short hike up to a massive glacier at the southern end of the park. A guide tells you that the glacier is made by snow that turns to ice and begins to move downhill. It will melt during the summer, feeding lakes and rivers. You strap metal spikes called crampons on your shoes and start out across the glacier. You pass huge cracks called crevasses. You see Sunwapta Lake, fed by the glacier and a river running out of it. On the drive home, you see that the river follows beside the road all the way back to town. You realize that you were swimming in glacier water at the river yesterday afternoon!

"Wow," you say when you get back to the cabin, "Thank you. That <u>was</u> cool!"

Logan says that he has to go pack and get ready for your hike the next day. You two will be walking the skyline trail with his dad and camping out for two nights.

Athbasca glacier

Hiking the Skyline Trail

HEADING OUT:

Logan and his dad meet you in the morning. They have a backpack for you already packed with some of the food and supplies you will need to carry for the group. All you have to do is pack your clothes in it. You pack layers to wear for the changing temperatures. You head north out of town in the truck, then make a right onto Maligne Road. Cross over a river and take a dirt road to your right. This is Signal Mountain Fire Road, where you will end your hike.

You park the truck here so it will be waiting for you. Logan's mom pulls up behind you. She will take you to the trail head. You load all the gear in her Jeep and go back to Maligne Road and take a right. You travel a long way, and you wonder how far you will walk to get back. You come to Medicine Lake and follow the Maligne River until the road ends.

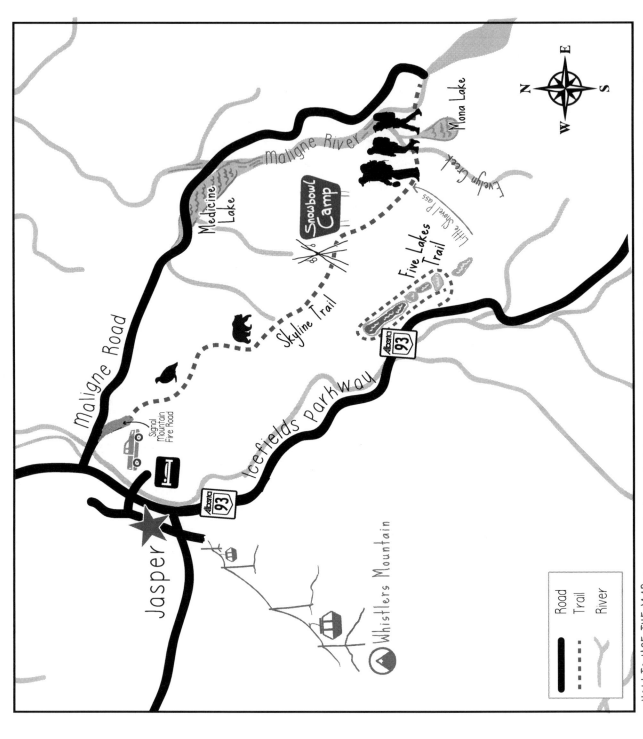

HOW TO USE THE MAP: Read each day's events. Follow along on the map finding each campsite. Pictures have been placed in the map to guide you. If you like, make notes or more small pictures where you spot more animals or landmarks.

Finally, you are out of sight. Your heart is beating wildly. You and Logan turn and start walking faster, looking over your shoulders to make sure the bear is not following you. You are safe. You choose another path to the lake, giving the bear plenty of room. You get back to the campsite and tell Logan's father the story. Logan says it was a grizzly because of its long claws. Logan tells his father that he forgot to take the bear spray from the backpack.

"There's nothing like meeting a bear to help you remember the bear spray next time. You should be proud of how you handled yourself, son," says Logan's father.

DAY 5: The next day is an easy hike back to the truck you parked at Signal Mountain Fire Road. You see a pair of ptarmigan along the way, but no more bears. You make it back to your cabin before dark. You thank Logan and his dad for a great adventure and say goodbye. The next morning, your family and Logan's family have breakfast together before you leave. You talk about your adventures and the memories you will have to share.

DAY 4: Start out early to cover a challenging 18 miles today and make it to Takkarra Campground. You cross big meadows before an easy climb up Big Shovel Pass. Then, it's downhill before a really hard climb up to the notch. There are very few plants now, mostly loose rocks and small patches of snow. Logan's father says that the snow doesn't melt here until July. You reach the top of the ridge, and the view is fantastic. You follow the ridge across barren ground. Down below, you spot a mountain caribou. Logan tells you that the mountain caribou are smaller than the tundra caribou. His dad adds that they only migrate to lower elevations in the winter instead of the long treks taken by the caribou on the polar tundra. Now it is downhill to the campsite. There is a lake, and you are happy to get rid of your pack as you settle in for the night. You and Logan head to the lake for some water. You come around a corner and see a bear, much too close. You freeze. Logan starts talking to the bear,

"Hey bear, we are just leaving now," he says as you both back away.
He keeps talking, "Hope you are having a good day, bear.
You can just get back to whatever you were doing—we'll be going now."

DAY 3: This is the trail head. Logan's mom wishes you happy trails as you disappear into the pine forest. The forest is full of lichens, mushrooms and mosses. It is not long before you reach the small Mona Lake and then, Evelyn Creek. There is a campsite there, but you are headed for Snowbowl Campground. You have miles to cover before the trail ends. You keep climbing up a gentle slope. You are in an alpine tundra. The plants are small and close to the ground. They bloom in reds and yellows. Even the rock is colorful with orange lichen. You come out of Little Shovel Pass, cross a valley and enter Snowbowl Campground. You set up camp for the night. There are some poles tied at the top like a teepee. After dinner, you tie the food up there for the night.

"Why?" you ask. Logan answers, "Bears."

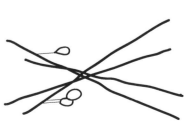

What if you met a bear?

Logan's father taught him to freeze if you see a bear. Look around to see if there are cubs or a fresh kill. You do not want to be between a bear and its cubs or its food. A mother bear will not usually attack once her cubs are safe. You should stand tall, look at the bear and back away slowly as you talk in a strong voice- not angry or scared. It doesn't really matter what you say. Never turn and run. If a bear follows you, pick up a stick. Have your bear spray ready to spray directly into its eyes, if it gets close enough. A bear attack is very rare, but it's always best to be prepared.

Write about what you would do if you met a bear.

_____

_____

_____

_____

_____

_____

_____

_____

_____

_____

_____

_____

Animal Research

Choose an animal of the Mountains of North America.
You can pick from your animals cards if you like. Draw and write about this animal.

Animal name

Class

Biome

_____

_____

_____

In 1960, glaciers in North America gained as much mass from snow as they lost in melt.

Find the year 1960 on the chart and go up the graph to the number 0. Find a circle where those two lines intersect, this is your starting point.

In 1965, glaciers in North America lost 3,000 cubic kilograms of ice. Find 1965 on the chart and go up the graph to the a place between 0 and -5 where you would put -3.
Make a mark where those two lines intersect.

In 1970, there were 4,000 cubic kilograms lost.
Make a mark on the line for 1970 just above -5.

In 1975, there were 5,000 cubic kilograms lost.
Make a mark on the line for 1970 at -5..

In 1980, there were about 7,000 cubic kilograms that melted
Estimate where to make your mark on the 1980 line.

In 1985, there were 10,000 cubic kilograms lost.
Make your mark on the 1985 line

In 1990, there were 17,000 cubic kilograms lost.

In 1995, there were 20,000 cubic kilograms lost

In 2000, there were 19,000 cubic kilograms that melted and made their way to the oceans.

In 2005, there were 23,000 cubic kilograms lost!
Use a ruler and connect the marks to show the rate of change.

What is happening to the glaciers?

The earth's climate is changing, due to the greenhouse effect caused by gases like carbon dioxide in the air. The average temperature all over the earth has increased by about one degree (F) in the past two hundred years. Alpine areas tend to warm even more. One result of global warming is that glaciers are melting. The change in the volume of ice in a glacier is measured by comparing the accumulation of snow and ice to the melting at the end of the glacier. A glacier can change with the seasons and still remain in balance. However, warmer temperatures, shorter winters and longer summers mean that more ice melts than snow accumulates. Then, the balance goes in the negative.

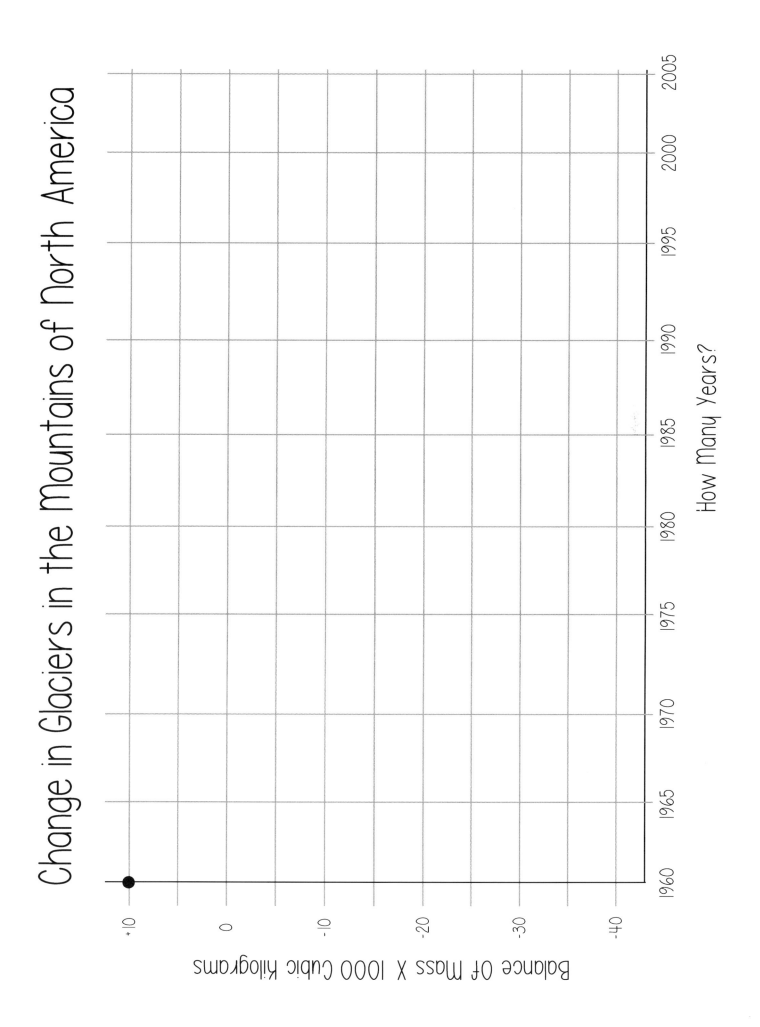

Draw a Trumpeter Swan

Use a pencil to draw the gray lines. Draw the black lines with a pen. Then erase the pencil lines.

Draw a pair of Trumpeter Swans in the rocky canyon lake on the next page.

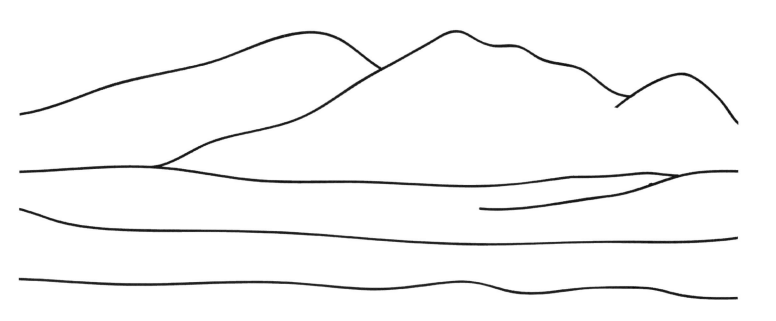

Adaptation Matching

The Mountains are colder and rocky at high elevations. Draw a line from the animal to the description of how it lives in its biome. Write a description of how the grizzly bear has adapted to life in the mountains..

bighorn sheep

This animal turns white in the winter and then turns brown and gray in the summer. It leaves the alpine tundra in the winter to go below the tree line. There, it finds plants to eat.

white-tailed ptarmigan

This animal is very busy just before winter, gathering piles of plants. It dries the plants in the sun before bringing them in to its rocky den. It has very thick fur.

pika

This animal has split hooves with rough bottoms to help it grip the rocky slopes. It has keen eyesight to help it see predators. It has fur that insulates it from the cold.

grizzly bear

_____

_____

_____

_____

Animal Research

Choose an animal of the Mountains of North America.
You can pick from your animals cards if you like. Draw and write about this animal.

Animal name   Class   Biome

_____   _____   _____

_____

_____

_____

_____

Mountain Food Chain

boreal toad

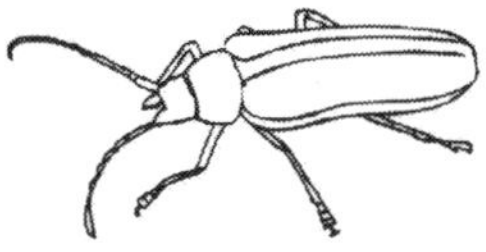

pine sawyer beetle

bristlecone pine

peregrine falcon

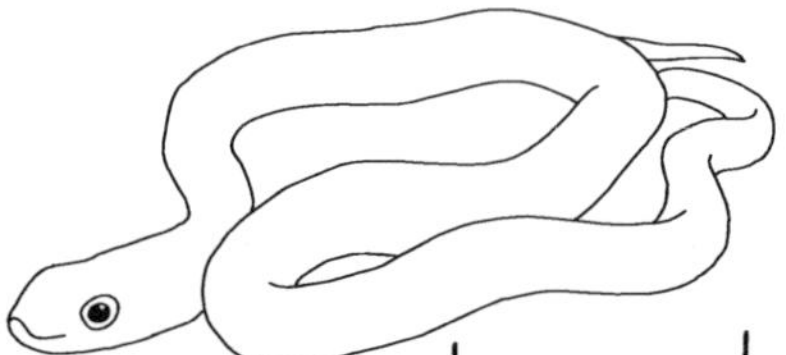

longnose snake

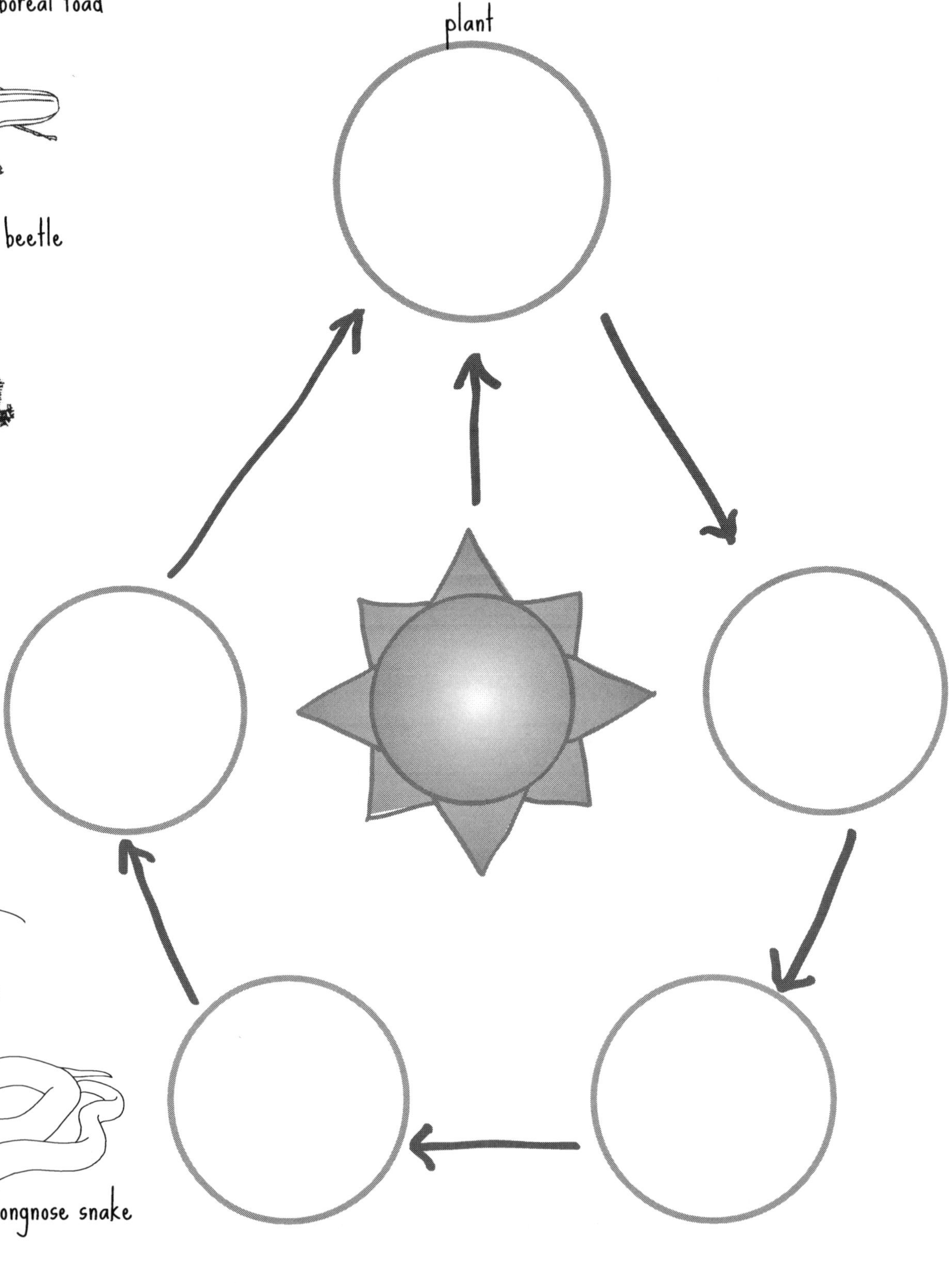

Start by drawing or writing the name of the bristle-cone pine in the circle for the plant that gets its energy from the sun. Follow the arrows to show the animal that eats the plant. Then, the animal that eats that animal. What eats that animal? What eats that animal? Draw it in the next circle. Use the animals illustrated.

plant

Plant Research

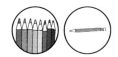

Choose a plant from the Mountains of North America.
You can pick from your cards if you like. Draw and write about this plant.

Plant name

Class

Biome

_____   _____   _____

_____

_____

_____

_____

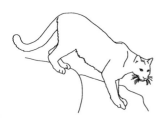

How Do They Interact?

Mountain lions and snowshoe hares live in the Mountains of
North America. The have a predator and prey relationship.
Draw their pictures in the right boxes.
Write their names underneath.

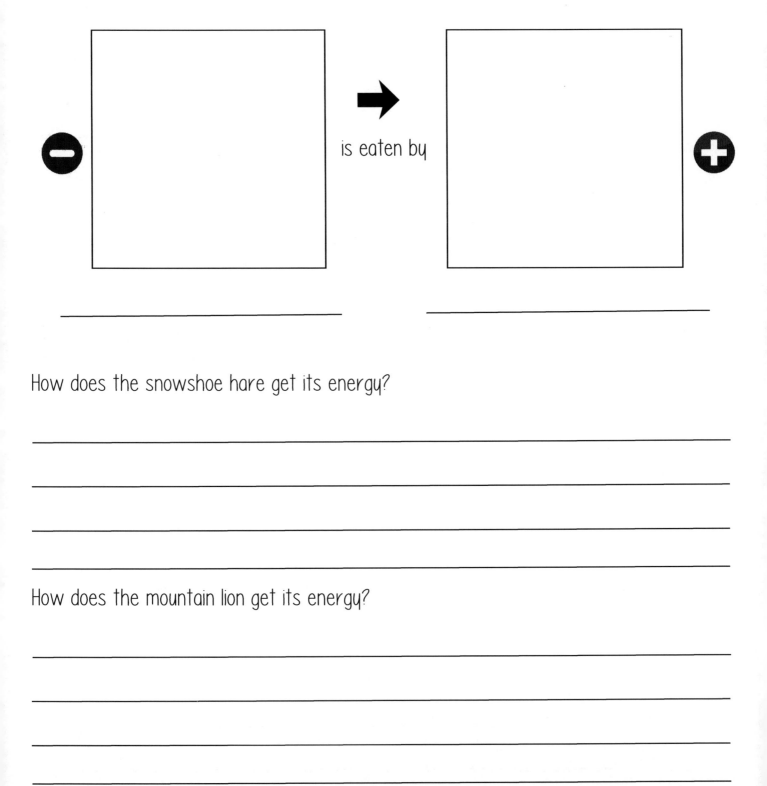

is eaten by

How does the snowshoe hare get its energy?

_____

_____

_____

_____

How does the mountain lion get its energy?

_____

_____

_____

_____

Animal Research

Choose an animal of the Mountains of North America.
You can pick from your animals cards if you like. Draw and write about this animal.

Animal name   Class   Biome

Things I know now about the Mountains of North America

_____

_____

_____

_____

_____

_____

Things I wonder about the Mountains of North America

_____

_____

_____

_____

_____

_____

On to the Polar Region of Kotzebue!

★ Kotzebue, Alaska

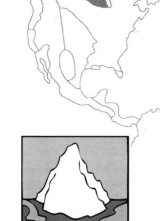

The Polar Region

This area covers the northern part of the continent. Ice covers the Arctic Ocean in the winter. The ground is frozen all year. Frozen ground is called permafrost.

Only small plants grow here. They may be very old, because they grow so slowly. Animals hibernate or migrate in winter.

Hello! My name is Oki! I live in Alaska. I am so excited to show you this wild and wonderful place I call home!

A Day In The Life Of Oki

snow	caribou, char and walrus	maktaq	polar region
midnight sun	snowmobile	seal or salmon	caribou	parka	umiak

Suvat! When I wake up, I feed our dogs, Nanuk and Sasha, then my brother

Malik and I eat breakfast. Most days, we eat cereal, but if my aaka

(grandmother) makes breakfast, we eat _____.

Sometimes, she'll sneak me my favorite treat, akutaq,

or "Alaskan ice cream"—berries mixed with whipped fat. Yum!

My mother drives me to school in a truck, but my brother likes to take the

_____ to explore the land.

I like to come with him and watch the wild

_____.

At school, I learn English, math, science, and Iñupiaq. Iñupiat culture is my favorite

thing to learn about. We learn about how our ancestors made sleds and

_____ , a type of boat from seal skins. We sing songs

and learn how to tell traditional stories.

At recess, we play outside in the _____.

If it's too cold, we play inside in the gym.

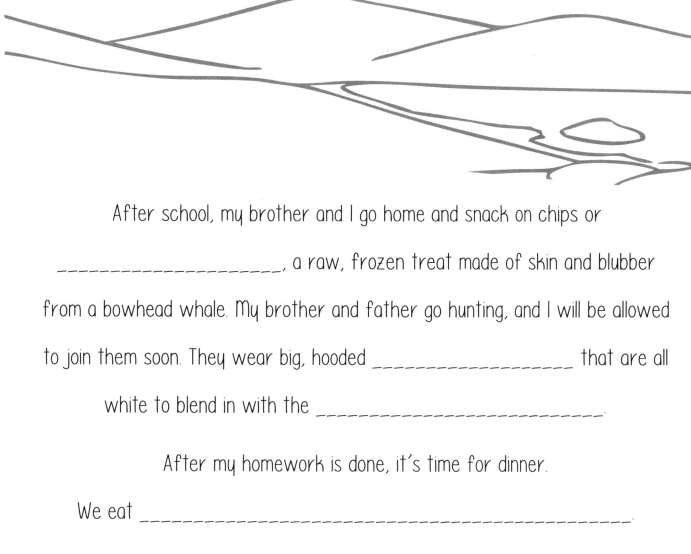

After school, my brother and I go home and snack on chips or

_____, a raw, frozen treat made of skin and blubber

from a bowhead whale. My brother and father go hunting, and I will be allowed

to join them soon. They wear big, hooded _____ that are all

white to blend in with the _____.

After my homework is done, it's time for dinner.

We eat _____.

Caribou is delicious, but it gets stuck in my teeth!

In the evening, we watch television or play games. My bedtime is 9 o'clock, but

it's not always dark—in the summer, we experience a month of

_____, when the sun shines all day and all night!

When it's time to sleep, we pull down the blackout shades on the windows

and snuggle under our blankets.

Unnuaqsatkun!

Adventures with Oki in Alaska

Oki has been your pen pal for almost a year now. Last week's letter was an exciting one. He wrote to tell you that the caribou herds would soon be migrating to the south before the winter. Watching this migration is fantastic! You showed this letter to your dad. He said, "I think it's time we go meet Oki and see the caribou for ourselves!" A call to Oki confirms your plans, and your dad books your flight to Anchorage, Alaska.

Dear Friend,
I can hardly contain my excitement! Winter is coming, and that means the caribou will be migrating south! It is a fantastic site to see, I wish you could come visit me. My brother and father and I will take our annual trip to take in the majesty of this event. I think you could visit? Pl...

Read the story on the next page and trace the course you took on the map.

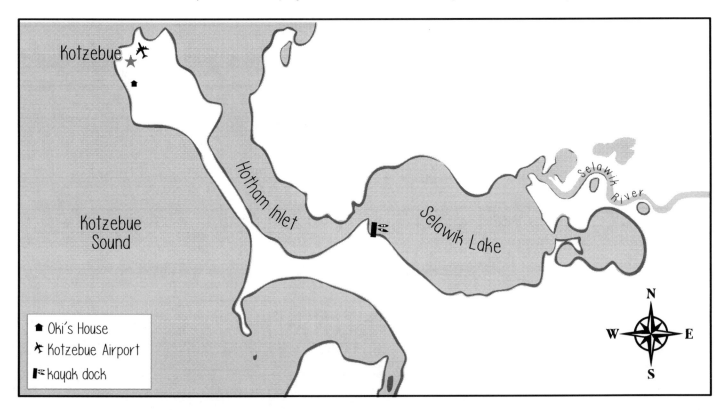

You fly into Kotzebue with your father from Anchorage. Oki is at the airport to meet you. You recognize him from the pictures he has sent you, and it is good to finally meet him in person. Oki's brother is driving the family truck. The three of you go to Oki's home for some caribou stew. After dinner, Oki tells you to get a good night's sleep, because they have big adventures planned for you this week!

In the morning, you dress warmly in layers, a parka, and boots. You go with Oki and his brother in the truck. From Kotzebue, you head southeast across an isthmus. You can see water on both sides of the road. You come to a small point of land where Selawik lake meets Hotham Inlet. There is a dock there. The boys know a man who lives here who has kayaks. He loans you and the boys two kayaks for the day. These kayaks are made of modern fiberglass, but they are shaped like the kayaks made by the Inuit.

Oki's 11-pound sheefish!

You take the kayaks out onto Selawik Lake. It is hard to see where the shore is, because there are grassy marshes along the edge. You paddle the kayaks to the northeastern shore where the Selawik River feeds the lake. The boys have brought some fishing gear. They tell you that Selawik is the Inupiaq word meaning "place of the sheefish". Sometimes, they come to the lake in the winter with their grandfather to fish through holes in the ice. Oki catches a large fish. His brother thinks it may weight 11 pounds! That is enough for dinner. Many of the people still live off the land and eat what they fish and hunt.

You take the way back close to the northern shore. Oki wants to show you a "pingo." You see a perfect dome-shaped hill in the distance. The boys tell you that a pingo happens when a pocket of water underground freezes and pushes the earth up as it expands. The ground is always frozen in the Arctic Circle. It is called permafrost. It is marshy when the ice and snow melts because the water cannot seep into the soil.

pingo

You dock the kayaks and drive back to Oki's house to have sheefish for dinner. His father says that he and the boys will take you and your father north to see the caribou herds migrating. His friends say this will be the week it happens. You learn that the herds always came in August, but each year now it is much later. They are worried that it is getting warmer every year. Tomorrow morning, you will leave very early on a bush plane, so get some rest!

The Migration of the Caribou in the Arctic Circle

HEADING OUT: Pack the bush plane in Kotzebue with all you need for the trip. The bush plane lands along the river bank just north of where the Cutler River joins the Noatak River. It is a rough landing over the uneven ground. The plane stops, and you hop out under the wing with your gear. You make plans with the pilot to pick you up in Noatak Village in seven days. It's late afternoon, so you make camp there for the night.

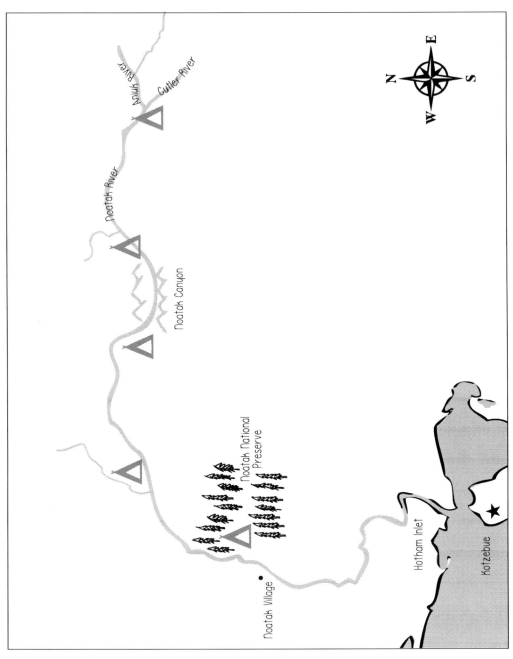

DAY 1: The next morning you pick wild blueberries to eat, get in the kayaks and float down stream. There is a lone wolf and a cub on the bank of the river. The adult slips into the brush but the cub comes to the edge of the bank watching us land on the opposite bank. You take his picture with your camera and paddle on. Later, you hear howling. Oki thinks it is the mother wolf saying, "You come home!" Make camp at the entrance of the canyon.

DAY 2: The next day, you spot two moose before leaving the flat river banks to enter the Grand Canyon of the Noatak. Oki points over to the top of a high bank where two Dall sheep are grazing. You paddle through the canyon and make camp for the night on the other side.

DAY 3: In the morning, you see 9 caribou swimming across the river just upstream. As you paddle the kayaks a few more miles downstream, you watch 2 musk oxen fighting across the river. They back up from each other and then spring forward, crashing their heads together. They have been at it for some time, and one of them seems to be winning the argument. It's getting dark, pull up onto the sandy riverbed and set up camp.

HOW TO USE THE MAP: Read each day's events. Follow along on the map finding each campsite. If you like, make notes along the map where you spot animals. Mark where you saw the caribou migration at its largest. Circle your first campsite and number the other campsites one through seven to track where you and Oki stay each night. You may stay at some sites more than one day.

DAY 4:

Before leaving in the morning, Oki's father shows you large prints around the camp. You guess that they are from a bear. You ask if it's a polar bear. Oki's father says "No, polar bears live closer to the Chukchi Sea, where they hunt the seals on the ice. The bears in the mountains are more likely grizzly bears. See the big claw marks in the tracks?" You are glad that they did not come into the camp and glad that the food was stored away from where you slept.

You are happy to get into your kayak and paddle downstream and toward the forest. You see a wolverine on the shore. It climbs a tree by the shore to get a closer look at you. He sees you and then runs away. You sight a group of three caribou before lunch and another six before you set up camp. That day, you spot a total of 14 caribou. Oki thinks that you might be getting close to the main herd.

That night you camp in a beautiful, mossy, dense forest. You've come out of the tundra now. As you set up camp, it begins to snow. Oki says that it will only be a foot or two deep, nothing to worry about. Two young caribou circle your camp that night, curious but shy. You and Oki eat jerky that Oki's mother packed for you. The wind is howling outside. The snow is still falling as you go to sleep.

DAY 5:

You wake in the morning to see the shadow of snow piled around the tent. When you unzip the tent and go outside, you see Oki's father waving at something moving towards you in the distance. As they get closer, you see that there are three sleds pulled by dogs! Friends are coming to give you a ride in the snow.

You travel east through the forest. Sitting in the sled with Oki, covered with furs the cold air is biting your face, but you don't care. You stop for lunch and then head back your camp in the woods. Along the way, you see 5 moose. Back at camp, the men fish and catch grayling. They are cooked over a fire that night. You and Oki feed the dogs raw fish from the catch and thank them for the ride.

DAY 6:

The next morning, you get up and walk outside to the edge of the forest. You hear the herd before you see them. It is like quiet thunder. Hundreds of caribou come into sight. All day, you watch the caribou. Now they must be in the thousands. You have given up counting. It is an amazing sight! Oki's father and brother go down to take a caribou with their bows. They bring the carcass back to skin and butcher it by the fire. The fur has grown thick before winter. The sky is very clear and you can see all the colors of the northern lights in the night sky. You stay at your camp site in the forest.

DAY 7:

In the morning, the caribou are mostly gone, but you see two huge tundra swans on the river. You pack up camp and paddle downstream and reach Noatak village. You are sad to see it because you know that means the end of a great adventure. You take the bush plane back to Kotzebue with the caribou, to make caribou stew and freeze the rest.

How many caribou did you see before you gave up counting?

_____

Estimate how many there were in all.

_____

Draw a puffin in its polar biome.

Draw the gray lines in pencil. Use a pen for the black lines.
Then erase the pencil lines and color your drawing!

Draw lots of puffins if you like!
Color the puffin by looking at the card and noticing its markings.

Layers of the Polar Tundra

Study the many unique layers of the tundra in these illustrations. Assign a different color to each layer. Fill in that color in the boxes on this page. You will find them next to the names of each layer. Now you have a key and can color all the layers together on the next page.

1. Ice and snow are found here most of the year. Perennial plants sprout in summer.

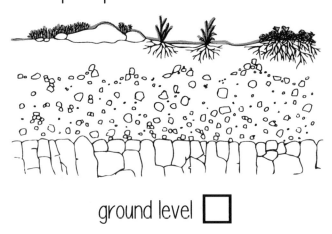

ground level ☐

2. Very wet in summer when the ice melts and cannot sink down into the permafrost.

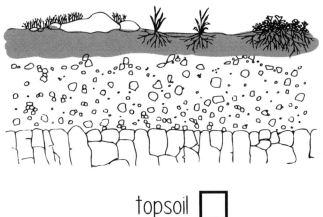

topsoil ☐

3. Permanently frozen soil and sediment.

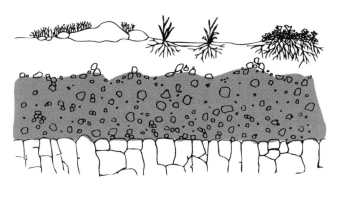

subsoil ☐

4. Made of unweathered, solid rock and sediment.

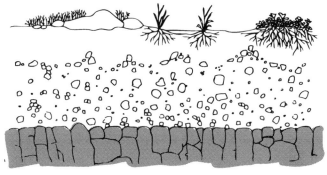

bedrock ☐

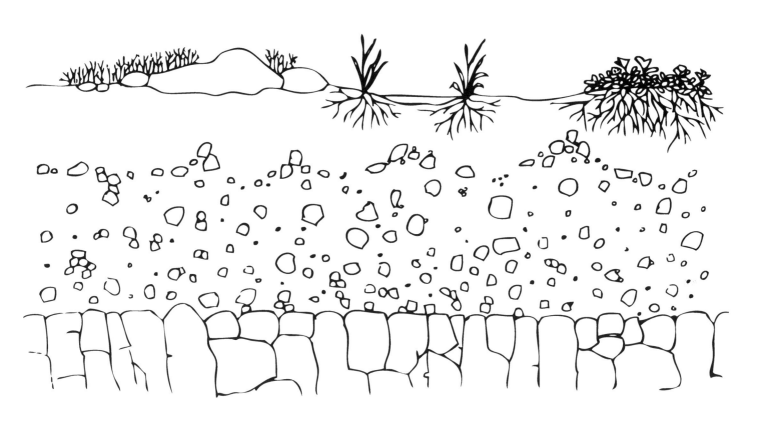

Musk Oxen Defense

In the frozen polar regions, it is June, and the snows are just melting. Baby muskoxen are born at this time. Wet from birth, they are in danger of freezing to death if they are not licked dry. The baby calf can stand soon after he is born. He stays close to his mother. They recognize one another by smell. Females only give birth every two years. Only a few calves survive each year. The whole herd helps to protect them. When the herd starts to move to new grazing, the calves must keep up. They stay in the middle of the herd as it moves. The musk oxen are large and heavy. Their hair hangs down long to the ground. They have hooves and curving horns. Finally, they come to a meadow where the snow has melted, with plenty of grasses and lichens to eat. They stop to graze. Sometimes, they raise their heads to sniff the wind for signs of danger.

A pack of wolves has spotted the herd from a hill not far away. They circle around until they are approaching the herd from downwind. This way, the wind doesn't take their scent to the herd. They crouch low and approach slowly. They are looking for a sick or old musk ox. When they don't find a weak one, they must try for a young one. The calves are in the middle of the herd. A bull gives a bellow of alarm when he sees the wolf pack.
The musk oxen quickly form a circle around the calves, facing outwards. Their horns are down low and they make a solid wall. The wolves come in and try to bite at them but their fur is so thick, they don't even feel it. One of the bulls rushes out and charges at one of the wolves. The wolf yelps and runs away while the bull runs quickly back to his place in the circle. The wolves circle the musk oxen but can find no way inside to the calves. Finally, they give up and walk away, looking over their shoulders from time to time. The musk oxen stay in their circle until the wolves are out of sight. The calves are safe. The herd goes back to grazing.

Why do you think the whole herd protects the babies?

_____

_____

_____

Why do the wolves look for a sick or old musk oxen? How could predators like wolves help a herd of oxen be strong?

_____

_____

_____

_____

Imagine that you are one of the animals in the story. You might be a mother oxen, a member of the herd, a baby oxen or a wolf. Imagine that you are that animal and tell the story the way that it happened to you.

Plant Research

Choose a plant from the Polar Region of North America.
You can pick from your cards if you like. Draw and write about this plant.

Plant name   Class   Biome

_____   _____   _____

_____

_____

_____

_____

How Do They Interact?

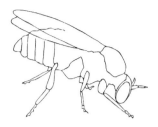

Black flies and lemmings live in the polar regions. Lemmings eat insects. Female black flies suck the blood of mammals. Draw their pictures in the right boxes and their names underneath. The arrows show how the energy moves.

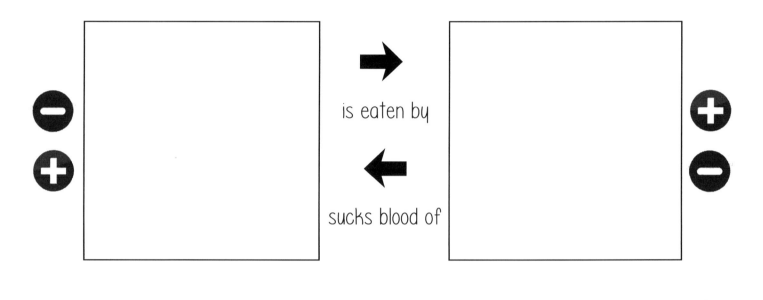

is eaten by

sucks blood of

_____   _____

How does the lemming get his energy?

_____

_____

_____

_____

How does the black fly get her energy?

_____

_____

_____

_____

How is the
Arctic Ocean changing?

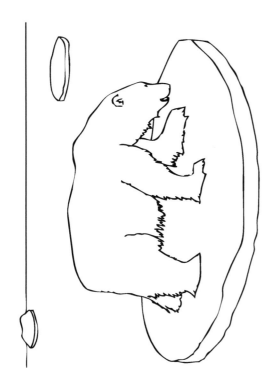

The earth's climate is changing due to the things that humans do, especially the burning of fuels like gasoline that put extra carbon dioxide into the air. The average temperature all over the earth has increased by about one degree (F) in the past two hundred years. In the Arctic, it is happening twice as fast. The ice is white and reflects the sun's heat. When it melts, there is no reflection and the water heats faster and the ice melts faster. As the ice melts, it will cause sea levels to rise all over the earth. Make a graph below to see how fast the ice is melting.

- In 1930, there were about 7,500 square miles of land area in the Arctic Circle. In 1978, there were about 8,000,000 square kilometers of ice in the Arctic Circle.
  Find 1930 on the chart and go up the graph to the number 8.
  Find a circle marked where those two lines intersect.

- In 1982, there were 7,500,000 square kilometers of ice. Make a mark on the line for 1982 just between 7 and 8 million.

- In 1986, there were still 7,500,00 square kilometers. Make a mark on the 1986 line just between 7 and 8.

- In 1990, there were about 6,300,00 square kilometers. Estimate where to make your mark on the 1990 line.

- In 1994, there were 6,800,000 square kilometers. Estimate where to make your mark on the 1994 line.

- In 1998, there were only 6,500,000 square kilometers.

- In 2002, there were 6 million square kilometers.

- In 2006, there were 5,800,000 square kilometers.

- In 2010, there were 5 million square kilometers

- In 2012, there were 3,500,000 square kilometers of ice!

- Use a ruler and connect the marks to show the rate of change.

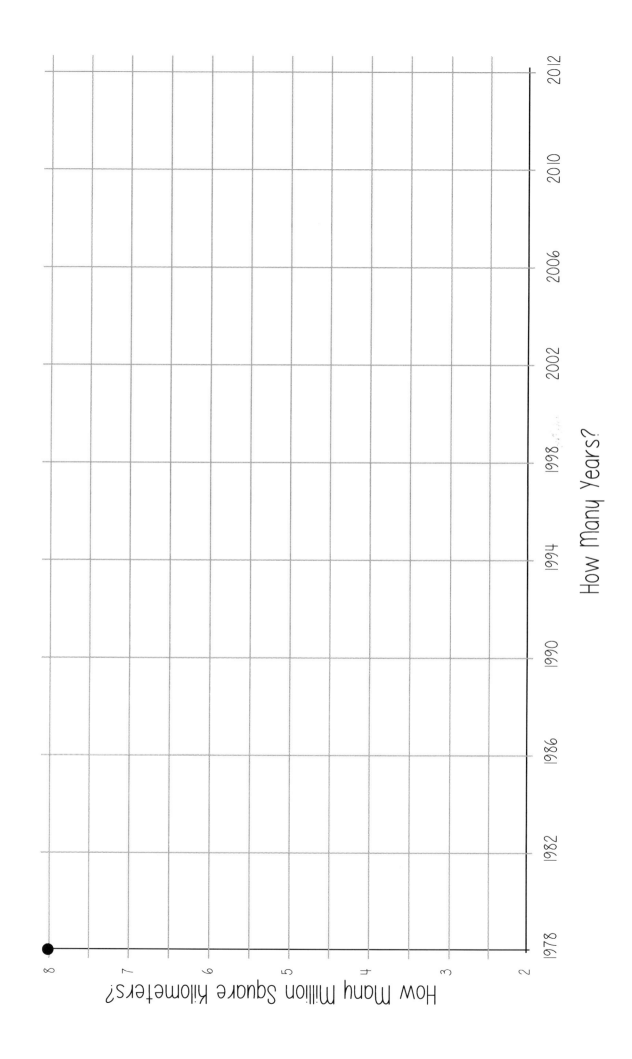

How Many Square Kilometers?

How Many Years?

2012 2010 2006 2002 1998 1994 1990 1986 1982 1978

Animal Research

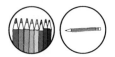

Choose an animal of the Polar Region of North America.
You can pick from your animals cards if you like. Draw and write about this animal.

Animal name   Class   Biome

_____   _____   _____

_____

_____

_____

_____

Polar Region Food Chain

Start by drawing or writing the name of the Arctic poppy in the top circle, for the plant that gets its energy from the sun. Follow the arrows to show the animal that eats the plant. Then, the animal that eats that animal. What eats that animal? Draw or write it in the next circle. Use the animals illustrated.

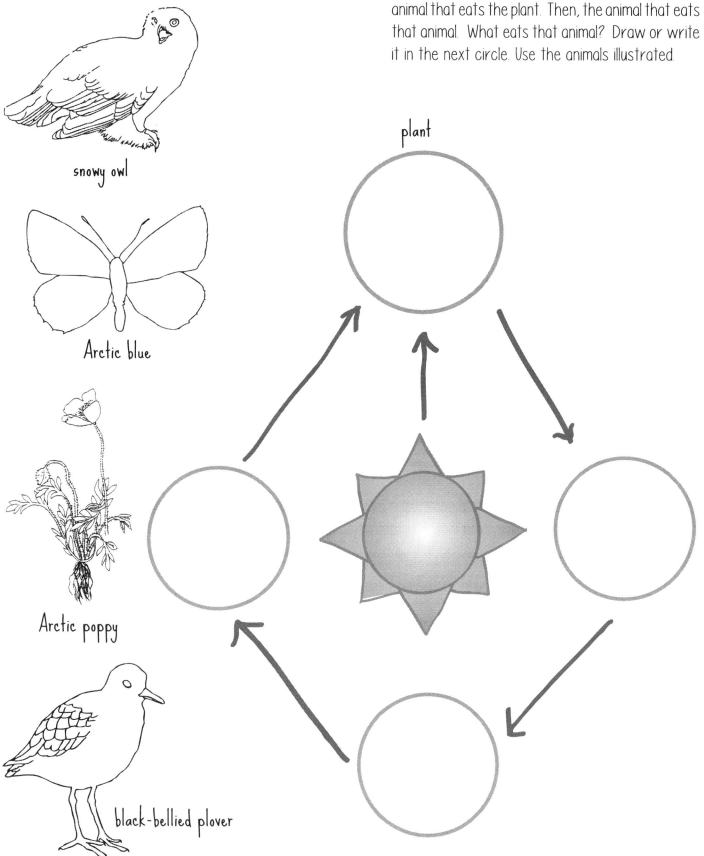

snowy owl

Arctic blue

Arctic poppy

black-bellied plover

plant

Animal Research

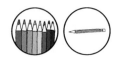

Choose an animal of the Polar Region of North America.
You can pick from your animals cards if you like. Draw and write about this animal.

Animal name   Class   Biome

_____   _____   _____

_____

_____

_____

_____

Parts of a Polar Bear

Draw a line from the adaptation to its purpose. Then draw in the biome around the bear.

small ears that can
open and close

grip on ice

thick layer of blubber

work like snowshoes
to distribute weight on ice

white fur

hunting and eating prey

furry feet

protect ear drums from
freezing water when diving

large feet

swimming and running

sharp claws and teeth

insulation and
store of energy

strong legs

camouflage

The Northern Lights

Since the beginning of time, people have told stories and legends to explain natural, but mysterious, things that happen. The Alaskan Inuit people believed the lights were the souls of salmon, deer and other animals.

The Northern Lights, also known as the Aurora Borealis, is the name of a beautiful light show of green, purple, pink, red or blue that appears in the night sky. They are best seen closest to the North Pole in the spring and fall.

Research some pictures of the Northern Lights and then use your colored pencils or chalk to draw the Northern Lights in the dark black Alaskan sky.

Things I know now about the Polar Regions of North America

_____

_____

_____

_____

_____

_____

Things I wonder about the Polar Regions of North America

_____

_____

_____

_____

_____

From Kotzebue to...

Let's go to your home town! Fill out this page with your current location.

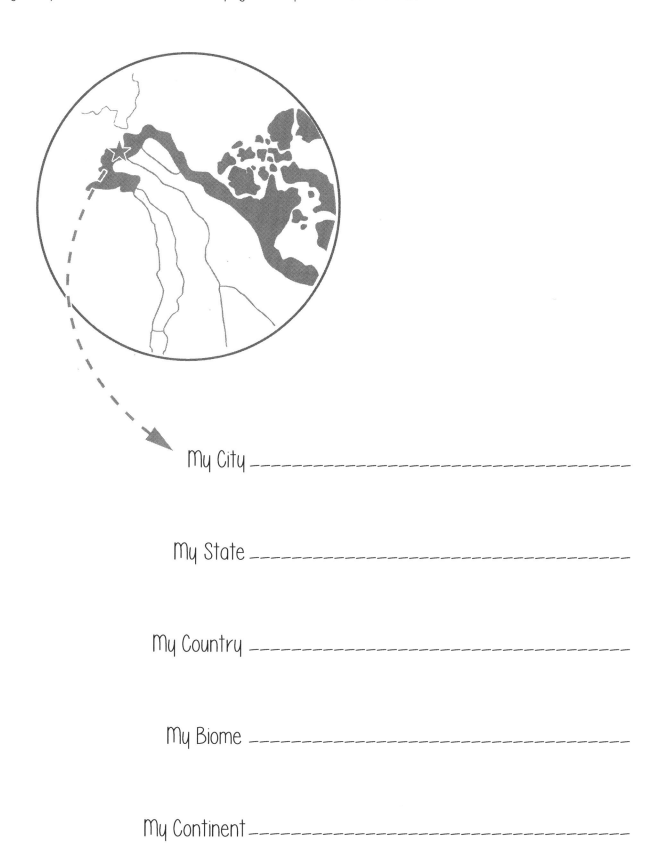

My City _____

My State _____

My Country _____

My Biome _____

My Continent _____

Write a letter

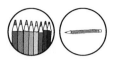

Choose one of your new friends from the biomes of North America. Tell them about things they taught you that you loved learning about. Tell them a few things about your home biome that they may think is interesting. Include a picture of your home in your letter. Invite them to come for a visit to your home.

draw your picture in here

Parts of _____

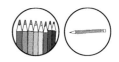

Draw a picture of your chosen species and label its parts. Write about any adaptations you learn about, too!

Make a Map

Your friend has written back to say they will come and visit! Make a map of a tour you will take them on.

A Day in My Life

In the morning, I wake up at _____

_____

_____

My school _____

_____

_____

After school _____

_____

_____

Before bedtime _____

_____

_____

Goodnight!

Growing up strong

Food and exercise can vary depending on your biome and culture.
How do your local resources feed and train your growing body?

Here are some foods I eat that are from my biome

EVERYDAY

SPECIAL DAYS

Here are some activities I do that keep me healthy

BY MYSELF

WITH FRIENDS

Happy Birthday!

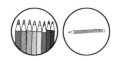

Celebrations for special days are very different for everyone. Use this page to write or draw about how you celebrate a birthday in your home, school or community.

Wild animals that I have seen in my biome

NAME	DESCRIPTION	LOCATION

Plant Observation

Explore the plant life around your home and record what you find. Pay special attention to drawing leaves, flowers or fruit. This will help to identify the species you have discovered.

DRAWING:

NAME: _____

LOCATION: _____

DESCRIPTION: _____

_____

_____

_____

DRAWING:

NAME: _____

LOCATION: _____

DESCRIPTION: _____

_____

_____

_____

The

End

Made in the USA
San Bernardino, CA
30 July 2017